MAKING PEG & DICE GAMES

MAKING BOARD, PEG & DICE GAMES

JEFF & JENNIE LOADER

Guild of Master Craftsman Publications Ltd

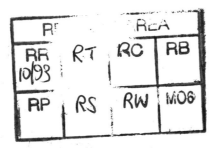

First published 1993 by
Guild of Master Craftsman Publications Ltd,
166 High Street, Lewes,
East Sussex BN7 1XU

ISBN 0 946819 40 8

Illustrations by Jeff Loader

All photographs not otherwise credited on captions are
by Eric Bignell

Designed by Gellatly Norman Associates.
Origination by Viscan Graphics Pty Ltd.
Printed and bound in Singapore by Kyodo Printing Co.

DEDICATION

To all our grandparents

ACKNOWLEDGEMENTS

We would like to offer our grateful thanks to the following people:

Suzette, Ray, Rowan, Ian and Barnabas for being there whenever needed.

Richard for the artistic baby-sitting!

Liz Inman and Ian Kearey from Guild of Master Craftsman Publications for all their support and encouragement throughout the production of this book.

Dr Helen Roberts for her perseverance and patience in keeping Jeff patched up!

Christie and Daniel for their support, and for just being Christie and Daniel.

G. Miller and Son, who have helped with our odd hardware requests over the years!

CONTENTS

Please note: throughout the playing rules for the games in this book, the pronoun 'he' has been used. This is purely for convenience and consistency; it is not our intention to exclude or offend lady readers!

INTRODUCTION

Games have been devised and played by man the world over, for many thousands of years. Man's ability to accept and enjoy an element of chance, along with his delight at challenge and the use of skills, is displayed in the wealth of games we are privileged to inherit.

Through the ages games have been developed to teach, to tell stories, to gamble, and just for fun. Wherever there is man you will find games, whether they are played with stones in the earth or hi-tech computers.

This book will enable you to construct and play some traditional games originating from different parts of the world, and some newly devised games which draw on both tradition and contemporary scenes for their inspiration. Children and adults alike will enjoy discovering and playing them.

Previous woodworking knowledge is not required; all the information necessary to produce the games as they appear has been provided. However, there are few rules and restrictions as to the way in which they are finished. Experienced woodworkers could incorporate marquetry, carving, turning and other skills, while the less experienced can experiment with colour and shape in order to add a personal touch to the finished games — ultimately the choice is yours.

Whatever you decide, with a little time, patience and care you will produce games that will be played and cherished for years to come.

If you enjoy playing games but do not wish to undertake any woodwork, you have not been forgotten — the majority of the games in this book can be produced using card, paper and shop-bought counters and dice.

Happy playing!

HOW TO USE THIS BOOK

LEVEL OF PLAY AND CONSTRUCTION COMPLEXITY: KEY TO THE SYMBOLS

On the first page of each game in the projects you will see the symbols of a die (Fig 1.1) and between one to three stars (Fig 1.2).

In Fig 1.1, the number of spots on the die's face

HOW TO USE THE CONSTRUCTION AND FINISHING INFORMATION

Chapters 2, 3 and 4, **'Construction Techniques', 'Board Marking'** and **'Colouring and Finishing',** provide all the basic information you will need to make all the games from start to finish.

Fig 1.1
Symbols for degree of game complexity.

indicates the complexity level of playing the game. One spot represents the simplest game, where the outcome is virtually totally dependent on luck, and six spots represents the most difficult in terms of skill. It should be noted that whilst some of the games' rules are easy to learn, their scope for strategic play is considerable. In these instances, the games level of play rating will be high.

The number of stars attributed to a game (*see* Fig 1.2) indicates the difficulty of construction. One star represents the easiest and most suited to the beginner, and three stars represents the most complex.

We suggest that prior to making any game, you first read through these sections and then refer back to them as necessary during the making process.

The additional, individual information required for constructing each game is to be found in the **'Construction'** and **'Marking and Finishing'** sections found under each separate project's heading.

Fig 1.2
Symbols for degree of construction complexity.

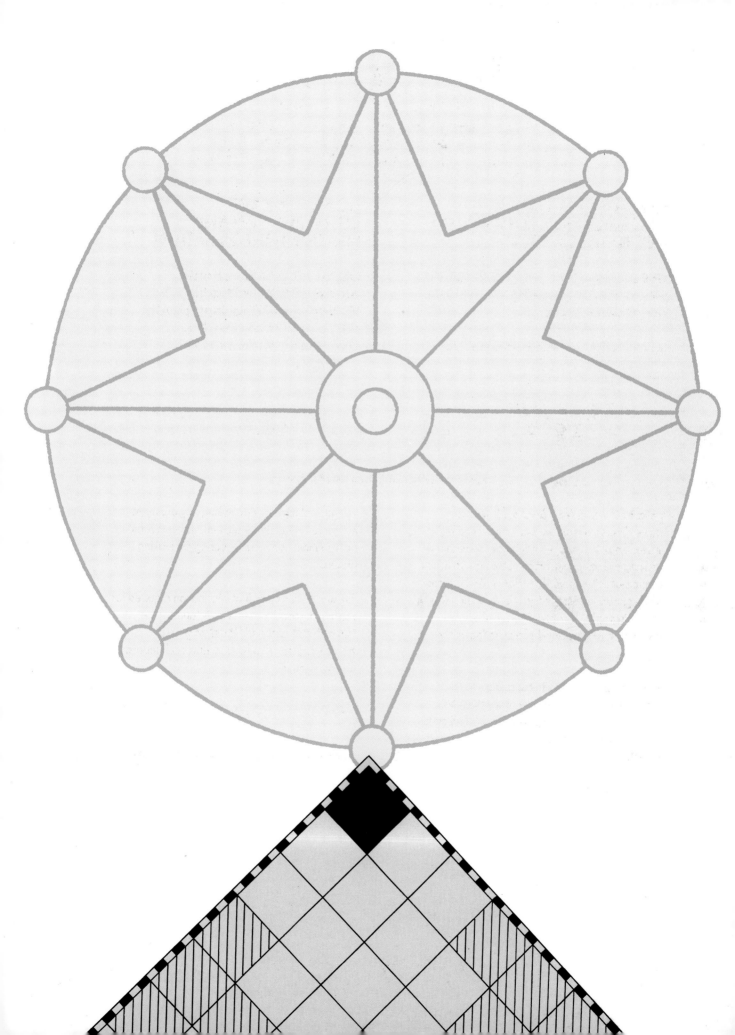

ALTERNATIVES TO MAKING THE GAMES FROM WOOD

Although all the projects have been designed for, and built from, wood, the majority of the games in this book can also be produced using card, paper and shop-bought counters and dice; there is no reason why non-woodworkers should not share in the enjoyment of playing the games too! In addition, initially constructing the games from card and paper is an ideal way of getting to know them before committing yourself to making them out of wood.

The game boards can be plotted out on to paper or card and coloured using paint, crayons, ink etc.

All the dice are six-sided, but their markings may differ from the standard numbers 1 to 6, depending on the game. To create the special dice, cover the sides of standard shop-bought dice with self-adhesive paper labels. These labels can be marked with any symbol required, using pen, pencil or transfers.

The playing pieces used in the games are very varied – pegs, horses, cars, ships etc. Counters, coins, buttons or tiddlywinks may be substituted in place of the originals. Again, coloured or marked self-adhesive labels can be attached to the counters to help differentiate between them. The horses, cars, boats etc. can be cut from card and made to be free-standing.

COUNTERS AND PLAYING PIECES

Each individual game will tell you what type of counters or playing pieces are required.

A few of the games will need counters for 'gambling': gaming chips, tiddlywinks, old coins, buttons etc. can be used.

Some of the game boards – Harry's Game (Chapter 23) and Crown and Anchor (Chapter 26) – have been designed with the intention that penny-sized counters would be used with them. These may be bought or simply made, by drawing around a penny on to stiff card and cutting out. Use different coloured card to denote different values of chip.

Certain games have specially designed playing pieces – the horses in Race Day (Chapter 21), the longboats in Viking Voyage (Chapter 22), and the cars in Motor Racing (Chapter 27) – which are fretsawed from wood. If you have difficulty in cutting these out, counters can be used instead.

If substituting counters for pegs, do remember there will be no need to drill peg holes in the board!

It is worth looking out for interesting objects that could be used as counters and playing pieces. For instance, the pieces used for Knights of the Round Table, Halma and Hnefatafl are, in fact, ready-made hardwood clock finials.

2
CONSTRUCTION TECHNIQUES

This chapter will provide you with guidelines for the construction of all the games. There is a descriptive list of the basic tools required, and techniques are given for constructing the actual game boards, applying the edging, and making pegs, playing pieces and dice.

It is not our aim to instruct you in general woodwork techniques, but to provide enough information to satisfactorily make the games as shown. Practiced woodworkers may use their own, additional skills to produce highly crafted work, possibly incorporating marquetry, carving etc.

MATERIALS

BIRCH PLYWOOD

All the game boards in this book are made from birch plywood. The fine, straight-grained structure of this material is ideal for marking the layout, for colouring and for varnishing. The grain pattern is also visually appealing.

Birch plywood is usually supplied in 2440mm (8ft) × 1220mm (4ft) sheets. When purchasing a large sheet, take your time selecting the right one for your needs; tell the timber merchants what you require it for and that you need the smoothest sheet they have. Try to pick one that does not have too many flaws. A good merchant will help you choose; they may also cut the sheet to the sizes you require, for a small extra charge.

If you are having your sheet delivered, make sure that you go to the timber merchants first, choose your sheet, and mark it so that you will know it as yours upon delivery – it may prove difficult to get the firm to come back and exchange the sheet if they send the wrong one.

The thickness of plywood used is controlled by

its suitability for both purpose and cost. 18mm (¾in) would be ideal, but is costly. 6mm (¼in) is considerably less expensive, but can be prone to warping (especially if used for the large boards) and is unsatisfactory if peg holes are required. Therefore, 12mm (½in) provides a happy medium.

To increase the 'visual thickness' of a game board, it can be edged with a deeper moulding or edging strip.

A few of the games, and some of the playing pieces, are made from a thinner plywood – 6mm (¼in), 3mm (⅛in), or 1.5mm (1/16in). As only relatively small amounts of these thicknesses are required, it is economical to buy small sheets from a hobby/craft supplier.

HARDBOARD

A small quantity of 3mm (⅛in) standard hardboard is required in the construction of one or two of the games. This is readily available from timber merchants and most DIY suppliers.

DOWEL RODS

The peg playing pieces required for some of the games are made from either 3mm (1/8in) or 6mm (1/4in) diameter ramin dowel rods.

Dowel is readily available from most DIY stores and timber merchants, although these sources may not stock the 3mm (1/8in) diameter size; this can be obtained from a hobbyist supplier.

EDGING

Lengths of moulding or edging may be applied to protect and enhance the edges of the game boards. Edging comes in an interesting variety of shapes, sizes and woods, and is readily available in strips. As it takes stain well and looks good left natural and simply varnished, the majority of the mouldings and edgings used in this book are made from ramin.

ABRASIVE PAPER

You will need an assortment of grades of abrasive paper, from medium to fine (100–150 grit). You will not normally require a coarse grade, as the majority of sanding will be done on the birch plywood, which should be relatively smooth when purchased; 60 grit can, however, be used for making dice. It is advisable to purchase a couple of very fine abrasive sheets (grade 00, grit 240) for final fine finishing.

Aluminium oxide paper and silicon carbide paper (known as wet-and-dry paper) are the ideal types to use.

WIRE WOOL

Wire wool is a useful item to keep at hand; 0000 grade may be used for lightly sanding a varnished surface prior to applying the final coat. It is also useful when applying wax polish.

GLUE

PVA adhesive (or 'white glue') is used for any gluing necessary in the construction of the games. It usually comes in conveniently sized bottles with a nozzle top.

PINS

Moulding pins are used with glue to fix the edging to the game boards.

Fig 2.1
**Selection of tools: hand drill and wood bits; pin
punches; awl; pincers and pin hammer.**

Photography by Jennie Loader

TOOLS

Some of the tools required to make the games in this book are listed below. Do not worry if you do not have all of them, as many of the games can be constructed with just a few.

Power tools and machinery are not mentioned (except for a power drill), because they are not essential for the construction of the games. If you do have power tools, they can, of course, save you much time and effort.

Whatever hand or power tools you choose to use, make sure that you know how to use them safely.

STEEL RULES

At least one 300mm (12in) steel rule, and preferably also one of 600mm (24in) will be required.

RETRACTABLE TAPE MEASURE

An excellent tool for measuring larger dimensions. A tape with a locking mechanism is preferable.

AWL

Used to mark the centre of holes before drilling, this is an invaluable little tool.

POWER DRILL COMBINED WITH VERTICAL DRILL STAND

Used to drill peg holes. A power drill held in a vertical drill stand enables the drilling of accurate holes. Its advantage over a hand drill is its vertical accuracy; the user of a hand drill, however careful, will inevitably 'slant' the drill slightly.

However, if a drill stand is not available, it is better to use a hand drill than a power drill used 'freehand', as the hand drill gives more control.

DRILL BITS

Twist bits can be used, but wood bits are preferable for drilling the peg holes – the central lead point and the two cutting spurs do not get deflected by the wood grain. Wood bits also produce a hole with a flatter bottom (*see* Fig 2.4).

ZIP BITS (ALSO KNOWN AS FLAT BITS OR SPADE BITS)

Useful for drilling a large hole. A zip bit used with a power drill is an effective and economical method. Each bit has a long central lead point that enables it to be fed positively through the workpiece.

Fig 2.4
Selection of drill bits: wood bits; zip bits; twist bits.

Photography by Jennie Loader

It is important to ensure that the ramin strip *is* actually square. Check this with a try square, and rectify if necessary, using a plane.

Working from one end of the strip which has already been checked for squareness, measure and mark on to the timber the length required for the die. Using the try square, draw a line around the timber at that marked point. Now, with the aid of a bench hook, saw the die part away. Continue this process for as many dice as you require.

The next stage is to clean up the end grain of the die (the part just sawn). If you are confident using a block plane, hold the die securely in a vice and plane the ends smooth. The end grain will split away if planed along the entire length in one stroke (Fig 2.11), so plane halfway from both sides (Fig 2.12).

If you do not have a block plane, or find it difficult to use on such small work, you can square the dice in the following way.

square. Periodically check the die with a square whilst gradually working down the grades of abrasive paper, finishing with a very fine grade.

A tip for checking squareness: when using the try square for checking squareness, hold the workpiece and the square together up to a light source. If any light can be seen peeping through between the bottom of the square and the surface of the work piece being checked, then it is not square. Where there is no light showing there is a 'high spot', which should be removed to square the surface.

Fig 2.11
End grain splits outwards when planed in one direction.

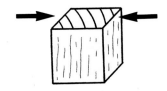

Fig 2.12
End grain will not split outwards when planed from both ends (stopping in the centre).

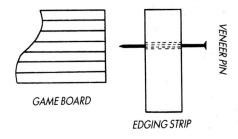

GAME BOARD

EDGING STRIP

VENEER PIN

Fig 2.10
Pinning edging.

Put a sheet of abrasive paper (graded according to the amount to be removed) face up on to a flat, smooth surface. Hold the die firmly in your fingertips and rub it on to the abrasive paper, using gentle circular strokes. It is important to keep the pressure on the die even, in order to keep it

Once you are satisfied that all the die's sides are square, the edges may be rounded off: wrap some abrasive paper around a small block of timber to produce a small sanding block. Hold the die in the fingertips of one hand, whilst rounding the edges with the sanding block. The degree of roundness is entirely up to you, but it must be even on each edge.

3
BOARD MARKING

The layout lines on each game board are marked with a black biro. These penned lines should be bold and slightly indented into the game board's surface.

This system of marking has been chosen because:
- it provides good, clear definition of the layout;
- the indentation produced by the pressure of the pen reduces the likelihood of the colour from one section spreading to an adjacent one;
- although requiring great accuracy, it is a straightforward method requiring no specialized equipment.

Considerable care must be taken when measuring and marking a games layout. Doublecheck every measurement before marking with the pen; this may be tedious, but once the lines are penned it is very difficult to correct any mistakes.

Fig 3.1
Selection of marking materials: steel rules; pencils; fine and medium black pens; craft knife; compass; French curves; circle template.

Photography by Jennie Loader

17

TOOLS REQUIRED

Steel Rules 300mm (12in) and 600mm (24in). You should ideally have two rules of each size, one for measuring and one for marking out the work; the reason for this is that over a period of time a small burr will be raised on the edge of the rule being used for marking.

Pencils We found 2H to be ideal, but anything from HB to 2H would be suitable.

Eraser

Black ballpoint pens We recommend Bic ballpoints with fine or medium nibs.

Circle template

French curves

Compasses

Fig 3.1 shows a selection of marking and measuring tools.

TECHNIQUE

After cutting and preparing the plywood game board, lightly mark out the required layout with a pencil.

Drill any peg holes required and lightly sand any roughness away from them. Re-mark any layout lines removed during this process.

Using the preferred biro size (fine or medium), mark over the pencil lines. Do not apply too much downward pressure to the pen; try to keep it running smoothly over the plywood. Use two or three such strokes on the same line rather than one heavy stroke, thus reducing the chances of error.

After completing a line, wipe the pen nib on a piece of scrap paper to clean away any ink build-up or wood fibres that may otherwise smudge the next line. The rule may also need the occasional wipe clean.

To mark curves and circles, use either French curves and/or a circle template.

When all the marking has been completed, erase any pencil lines still showing. Any really stubborn marks can be removed by very light sanding with a fine grade of abrasive paper (60 grit).

4
COLOURING AND FINISHING

MATERIALS AND TOOLS

ACRYLIC PAINTS

Acrylic paints are available in two types: artist's and hobbyist. Both types are water-based. The artist's paints come in tubes and have a thick, creamy consistency. Hobbyist paints, available in matt and gloss finishes, come in small pots and are more liquid. Both types may be used for painting or, when mixed with water, staining.

HOBBYIST/MODELLING ENAMEL PAINTS

Enamel paints are oil-based, available in both matt and gloss finishes, and come in small tins.

WOOD DYES

Ready-mixed wood dyes are available in a wide range of colours, and can be spirit- or water-based. These stains are especially good for their 'natural' wood colours such as walnut, mahogany, oak etc.

OTHER COLOURING MATERIALS

The above list is by no means finite. Experiment with other forms of colouring mediums if you wish e.g. inks, other paints etc. *See* Fig 4.1 for a selection of colouring and finishing materials.

Fig 4.1
Selection of colouring and finishing materials: artist's and hobbyist's acrylic and enamel paints; paintbrushes; varnish.

Photography by Jennie Loader

19

VARNISH

Ready-to-use polyurethane gloss varnish has been chiefly used on the games shown in this book. This versatile varnish is also available in matt and satin finishes.

A drawback to using this type of varnish is that over a period of time it tends to 'yellow'. Although this 'yellowing' may actually add appeal to some game boards, providing the effect of ageing, to avoid it, use a super clear modelling varnish. This will not 'yellow', and is also available in matt, satin and gloss finishes.

AUTO SPRAY CLEAR LACQUER

Traditionally cellulose-based, this lacquer is now also available in acrylic (water-based) form. It comes in aerosol cans, dries quickly and gives a very even, smooth finish. Either type may be used as an alternative to polyurethane varnish.

BRUSHES

There is a huge variety of brushes on the market, and which make, size and style you choose to use is really a matter of personal preference. However, always go for good quality; it is false economy to buy cheap brushes – they will not last, and a satisfactory finish will be harder to achieve.

Only a few brushes will be required for finishing the games shown in this book (*see* Fig 4.1). Try to use separate brushes for acrylics and enamels. Brushes used for varnishing should not be used for painting or staining. Store the brushes upright in pots; it is useful to have a separate pot for each set of brushes.

WHITE SPIRIT

White spirit is used for thinning and cleaning oil-based paints and varnishes.

Photography by Jennie Loader

PALETTE

A palette on which to mix paints and stains will be necessary, and an old white plate or clean plastic lid from a margarine tub can be used for this purpose.

TRANSFERS

Most of the lettering, numbers and symbols found on the game boards and the dice are transfers of the dry rubdown variety. Good stationers and graphic art suppliers usually stock a wide range of styles and sizes.

These transfers are simple to apply and so thin that they blend with the workpiece completely, leaving no raised edges.

It is possible to cut and join the transfers to make up symbols of your own, and an example of this is the dice for Crown and Anchor (Chapter 26). Of course, you can paint the relevant symbols yourself, but this will take time, patience and a very steady hand!

Other types of transfers and stickers may be used, but they do have certain drawbacks. For example, the waterslide variety tends to be messy to use and leaves a fine film around the edge of the symbols.

Whatever system of lettering, numbers and symbols you choose to use, you will need to apply one or two protective coats of varnish over the top. Check beforehand that the type of varnish you use does not react with the transfers.

VELOUR

Self-adhesive velour, with its nylon pile, provides an excellent covering material for the base of the game boards. Used on the base of the playing pieces and counters, it will also protect the playing surface of the game boards.

Velour is simple to use, and has the advantage of being removable should a piece be applied incorrectly. It is readily available in roll or sheet form from most hardware stores and hobby suppliers.

To apply, cut a piece slightly larger than the area you wish to cover. Peel away the backing paper and apply to the required area, then press the velour down evenly and trim any surplus with a craft knife.

SELF-ADHESIVE PLASTIC COVERING

As an alternative to wooden edging, wood-effect self-adhesive covering may be used.

TECHNIQUES

COLOURING

Before starting on a game board, it is advisable to practise using your mediums and techniques on some scrap pieces of plywood.

Make sure that these test pieces are sanded smooth, and draw a few lines on them with a rule and ballpoint, ready to practise applying stain, paint or varnish up to and along the lines (*see* Fig 4.2).

Test the colour and density of your chosen medium. Remember that you can always darken a lightly stained piece of work, by restaining it with the same or a slightly darker mix, but you cannot easily lighten a darkly stained area. Also bear in mind that you are colouring wood, so you want to highlight, not obliterate, the grain. This may seem an obvious point to make, but it is easy to get carried away with using too many dark and rich colours.

Most of the bright stained colours used on the game boards in this book are thinned acrylic paint (either artist's or modeller's matt). The beauty of using this type of paint is that you can thin it with water to the consistency that suits you. It will thus stain, not paint, the wood, allowing the wood grain to show through.

Whatever medium you use, ensure that it is colourfast. It would be a great pity to have lavished hours of care making a game, only to have the colours fade away!

The majority of staining required will be on small areas, so a brush is the best implement to use. Experiment with different types and techniques of

Fig 4.2
Testing out different finishes, colours and marking techniques on a scrap piece of birch plywood.

Photography by Jennie Loader

brushing, but above all, be confident and enjoy it – this is one of the most satisfying tasks in the construction process.

The one golden rule is to work cleanly. Make sure that your workpiece and environment are as clean and dust-free as possible, and always work with clean hands and implements.

After colouring, it may be necessary to re-line some of the penned lines which you have stained over.

MASKING AREAS

Colouring a game board entirely one colour – for instance, End Zone (Chapter 19) and Soccer (Chapter 17) – is straightforward. However,

staining a board with more than one colour may make it necessary to 'seal' certain areas. Even when the areas are separated by indented penned lines, a colour may still creep along the wood grain into the adjacent area. This especially happens when using wood dyes, which tend to creep more than thinned acrylic paint stain. Obviously this creeping is undesirable, especially when you wish to leave some areas natural.

To seal an area, simply apply one or, preferably, two coats of clear varnish to that area. Do not thin the varnish, as this may cause it to creep to an area which you wish to colour!

This technique can be practised on scrap plywood; pen some squares, seal some and colour others.

VARNISHING

After colouring a game board, it is best to protect the surface with varnish – dice, counters, pegs and regular use will otherwise eventually wear and mark it.

Apply the varnish with a clean, soft-bristled brush. Do not overload the brush and do not wipe it on the rim of the can, as this will create small air bubbles that will transfer to the surface of the game board.

Spread the varnish evenly in different directions, finishing with light, 'laying off' strokes in the direction of the wood grain. Do this in small sections at a time on a large game board. When varnishing near an edge, always brush towards the edge to prevent any surplus running down the sides.

We recommend that at least six coats of varnish be applied to a game board. It goes against the rule book, but it is better **not** to sand the game board between the first few coats. This is because sanding may damage the design, especially on an intricately coloured board. Lightly sand between the final coats with a combination of very fine abrasive paper and 0000 grade wire wool.

Gloss varnish offers greater protection than matt or satin. If you prefer these latter finishes, use a gloss varnish for the first few coats, followed by matt or satin for the last two.

If unsightly dust particles land on the final coat of varnish, these can be removed by rubbing the surface with some 0000 wire wool loaded with a suitable wax polish. Burnish with a soft cloth, working with the grain.

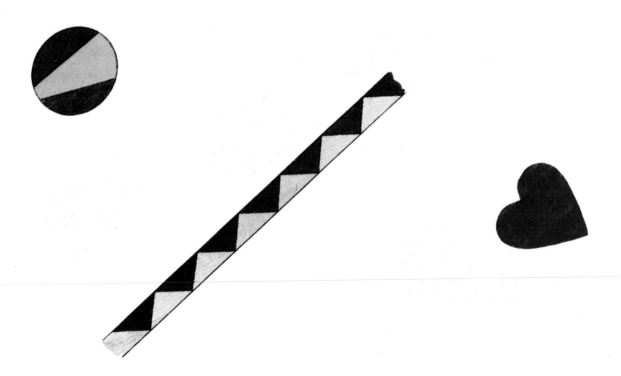

Do not wax anything until the edging, if used, has been applied, and the top coat of varnish has been applied to both the game board and edging. Varnish will not take over wax!

If you choose to use an aerosol lacquer, follow the manufacturer's directions fully. Beware of spraying the aerosol lacquer over any previously applied polyurethane varnish; in some instances the lacquer may react with the varnish (and also with some paints) and ruin the finish. Test on a scrap piece before use.

APPLYING COLOUR OVER VARNISH

At first this may appear to be a contradiction in terms, but there are instances when this technique is useful, e.g. the Knights of the Round Table (Chapter 29). After the first two coats of varnish, it was evident that the blue colour was not strong enough, so a subsequent thinned coat of acrylic paint was applied on top of the varnish.

When doing this, care must be taken to achieve the correct consistency. Too thick, and it will cover up the grain; too thin, and it will not adhere to the varnish properly (if you are using a water-based medium). Further coats of varnish may be applied when the stain is dry.

Another situation where this technique may be useful is when applying a dense colour, e.g. the black on the Mu-Torere game board (Chapter 9). Instead of masking the areas to be left natural, it is quicker to varnish the complete board and then apply the black over the varnish in the required areas. Finish the game board, as you would after any other colouring process, with a couple of coats of varnish.

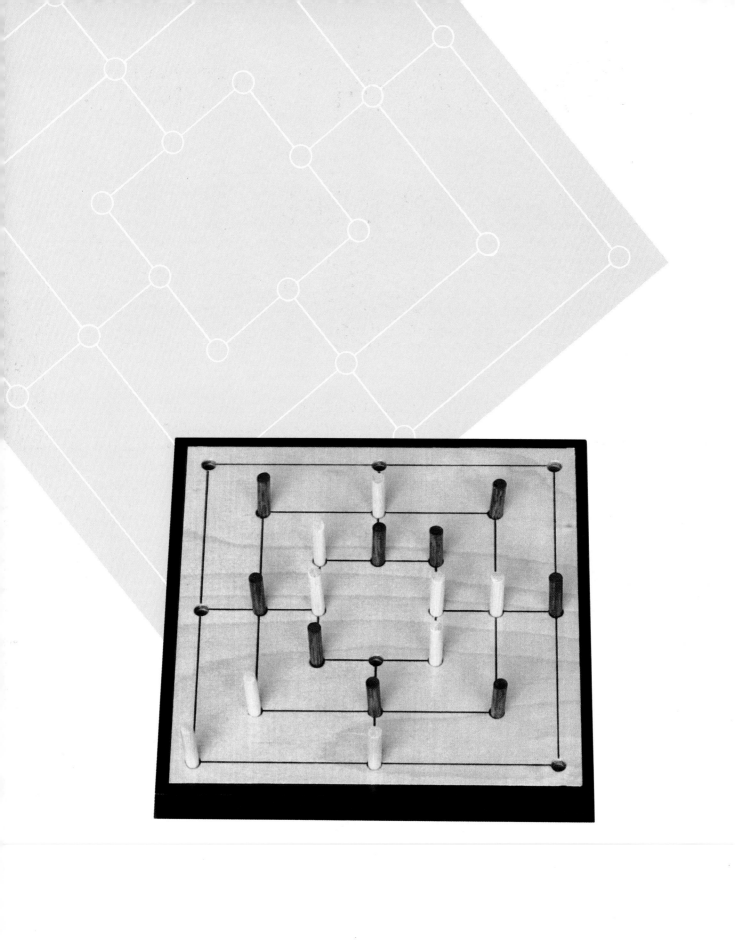

ΠINE MEN'S MORRIS

INTRODUCTION

Nine Men's Morris, also known as Merelles in France and Mill in Germany, is probably one of the oldest and most popular board games in the world. There is evidence of the game being played from Ancient Egyptian times to the present day; it is still played throughout the world, and has many variations and derivatives.

The game shown here is a peg board version. If preferred, you could use counters instead of pegs and simply omit the peg holes.

OBJECT OF THE GAME

To reduce your opponent's playing pieces from nine to two, or to immobilise them by blocking the pegs so he is unable to move.

FOR TWO PLAYERS

EQUIPMENT

- ● Nine Men's Morris game board
- ● Nine light pegs, nine dark pegs

PLAY

Play is divided into two distinct stages.

First stage
Each player has nine pegs of his own colour. Taking it in turns, each player must place one peg into a vacant hole on the board. If a player forms a row of three of his own pegs (called a mill), he may remove one of his opponent's pegs from the board. Pegs which are in a mill may not be removed.

Second stage
When all 18 pegs have been put into play, each player takes turns to move his pegs (one per turn) to an adjacent, vacant peg hole. The pegs may only be moved along the lines.

As in the first stage, players are trying to form a mill (three in a row) and therefore attempt to remove an opponent's peg. Again, any pegs in a mill may not be removed.

A mill may be broken (a peg moved away) and then reformed (the same peg moved back again on the next move) any number of times.

When a player has reduced his opponent to two pegs, he has won the game. Alternatively, a player may also win by blocking the pegs of the other player so that he is unable to move.

CONSTRUCTION

Game board 12mm (½in) birch plywood 170mm (6¹¹⁄₁₆in) × 170mm (6¹¹⁄₁₆in).
Edging 17mm (¹¹⁄₁₆in) × 5mm (⁷⁄₃₂in) ramin strip.
Peg holes 6mm (¼in) diameter, drilled at every line intersection point – 24 in total.
Pegs Eighteen 30mm (1³⁄₁₆in) long pegs.

MARKING AND FINISHING

All lines are penned.

The board is left natural and varnished.

The edging is painted black and varnished.

Nine of the pegs are left natural, and nine are coloured using a dark shade of wood dye.

Fig 5.1
Nine Men's Morris game board.

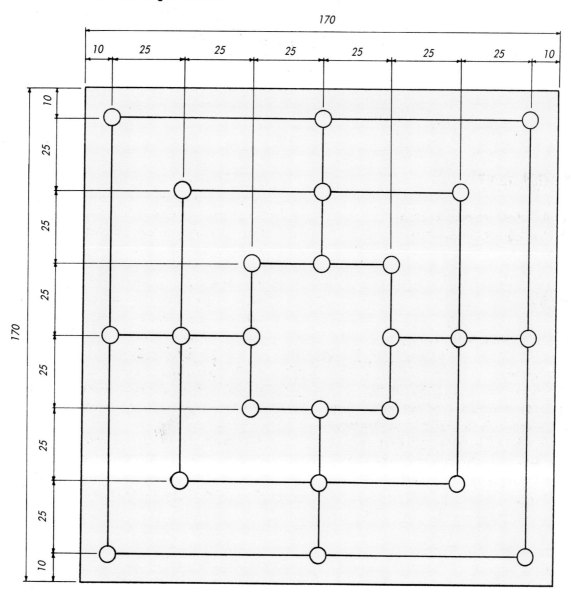

29

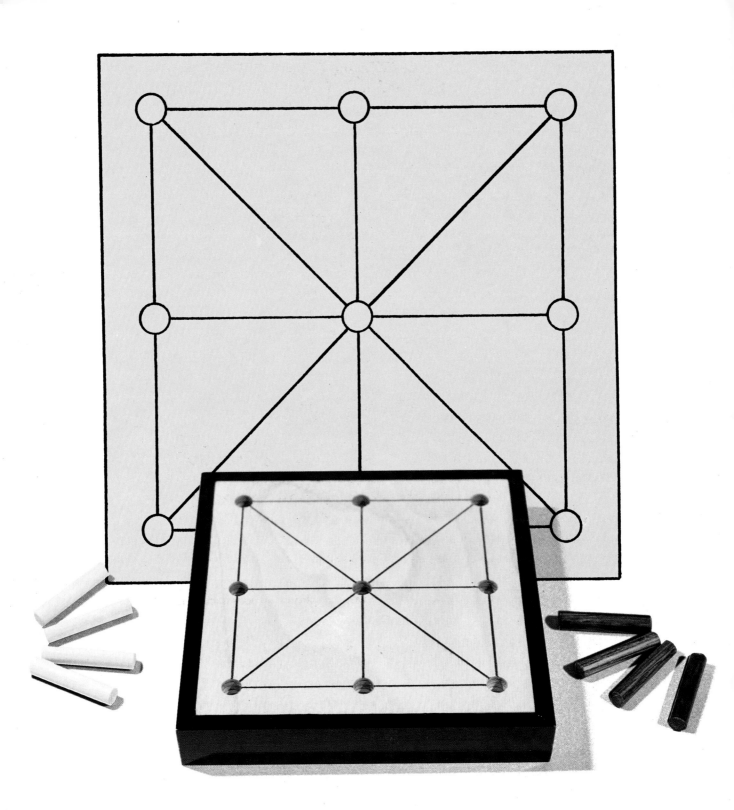

ACHI

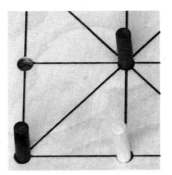

INTRODUCTION

Achi originates from Central Africa, where it is often played on a board marked out on the ground (*see* Fig 6.1). Sticks and stones are used for playing pieces. It is one of the many games akin to Nine Men's Morris which have maintained popularity for hundreds of years.

OBJECT OF THE GAME

To be the first player to position three playing pieces in a row.

FOR TWO PLAYERS

EQUIPMENT

- Achi game board
- Four light pegs, four dark pegs

PLAY

Taking it in turns, each player places one peg at a time into any empty hole on the board.

When all eight pegs have been placed on the board, the players, again in turn, each move a peg along the lines to a vacant hole. Play continues in this way until one player has obtained a row of three pegs, thus winning the game.

CONSTRUCTION

Game board 12mm (½in) birch plywood 100mm (4in) × 100mm (4in).

Peg holes 6mm (¼in) peg holes are drilled at every point where the marking lines intersect.

Edging 21mm (1³⁄₁₆in) × 5mm (³⁄₁₆in) ramin strip.

Pegs Eight 30mm (1¼in) × 6mm (¼in) dowel pegs.

MARKING AND FINISHING

The playing area is left natural and varnished.

The ramin edging is painted black and varnished.

Four of the pegs are stained a dark brown, and four are left natural.

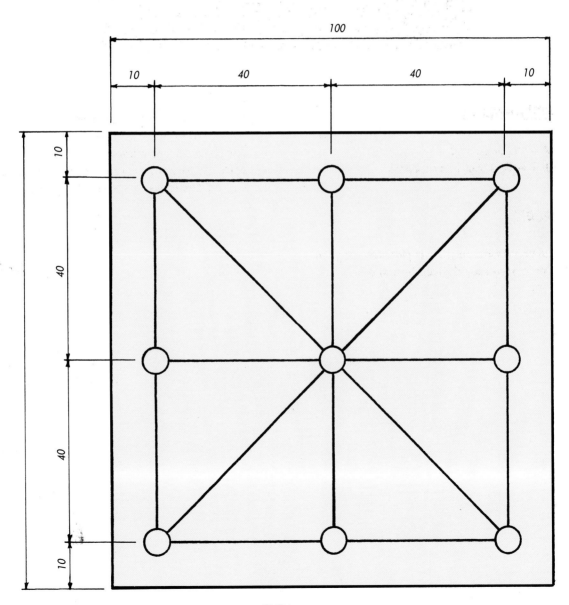

Fig 6.1
Achi game board.

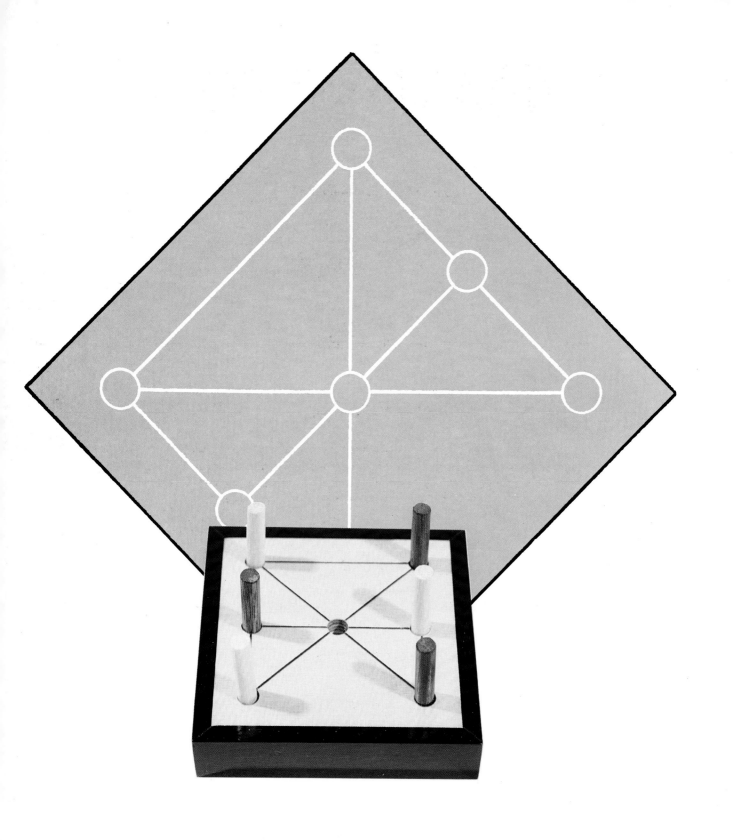

MADELINETTE

INTRODUCTION

Madelinette is very similar in format to the game of Pong Hau K'i, which is played in Canton, China. Although played on a similar grid pattern, it differs in that it has six pegs as opposed to four pegs in Pong Hau K'i and therefore provides a greater challenge.

OBJECT OF THE GAME

To block your opponent's pegs so that he is unable to move.

FOR TWO PLAYERS

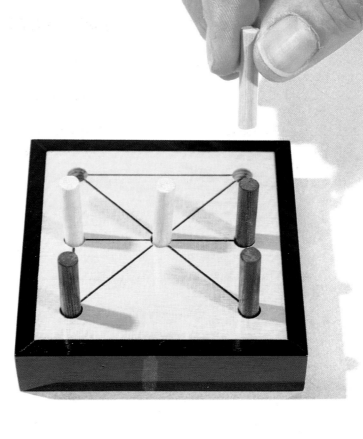

EQUIPMENT

- Madelinette game board
- Three light pegs, three dark pegs

PREPARATION

The pegs are positioned on the board as shown in the photograph on page 34. One player controls the three light pegs, the other player controls the three dark pegs.

PLAY

The game starts with one player moving one of his pegs along a line to the vacant hole in the centre of the game board.

The other player then moves one of his pegs along a line to the vacant hole.

Play continues in this way, with turns alternating, until one player has blocked the other so that he is unable to move any of his pegs.

ALTERNATIVE METHOD OF PLAY

The pegs need not be placed in a set position at the start of the game, but may be placed by the players, taking alternate turns, into positions of their choice. Play then continues as described above.

CONSTRUCTION

Game board 12mm (½in) birch plywood 70mm (2¾in) × 70mm (2¾in).
Edging 17mm (¹¹⁄₁₆in) × 5mm (³⁄₁₆in) ramin strip.
Peg holes Seven 6mm (¼in) holes are drilled at every point where the lines intersect.
Pegs Six 30mm (1³⁄₁₆in) × 6mm (¼in) dowel pegs.

MARKING AND FINISHING

The game board is left natural and varnished.

The edging is painted black and varnished.

Three pegs are left natural, three are stained a dark brown using wood stain.

Fig 7.1
Madelinette game board.

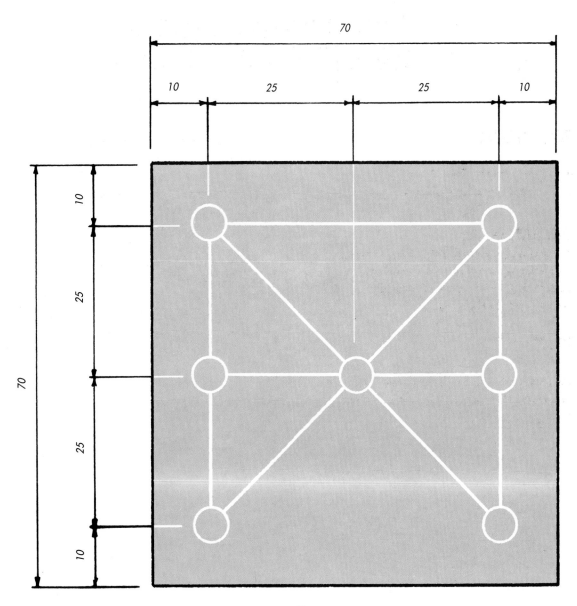

37

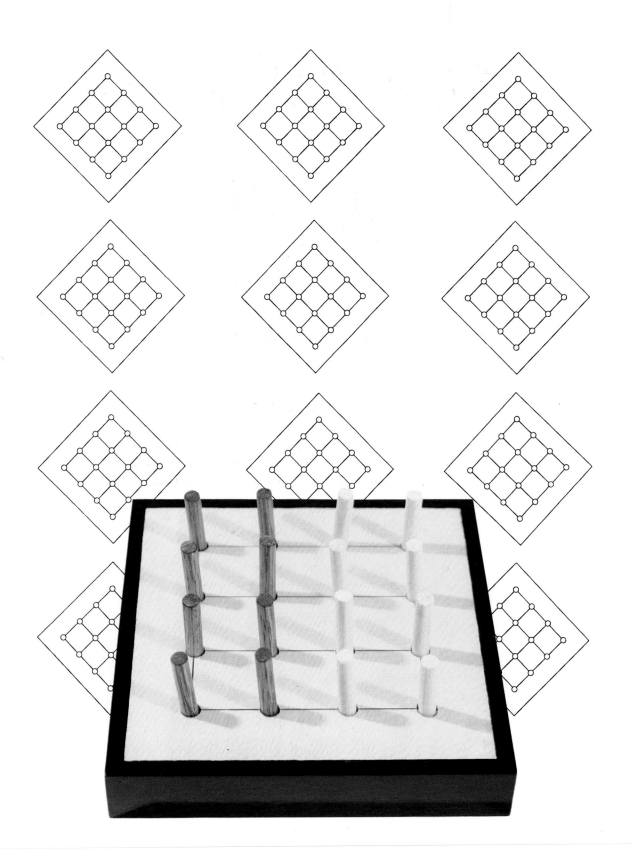

FOUR FIELD KONO

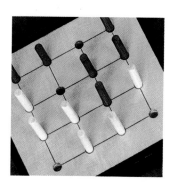

INTRODUCTION

This traditional game requires careful strategy in order to
successfully beat your opponent. It comes from a family of
games which also includes the Korean game of Five Field Kono.

OBJECT OF THE GAME

For each player to capture his opponent's pieces, or to block
them so that they are unable to move.

FOR TWO PLAYERS

EQUIPMENT

● Four Field Kono game board
● Eight light pegs and eight dark pegs

PREPARATION

One player controls the light pegs, and one the dark pegs. Each player places all his eight pegs into the two rows of peg holes directly in front of him.

PLAY

To capture an opponent's peg, a player must jump one of his own pegs over another of his own pegs on to the opponent's peg. The captured peg is removed from the board, and the victorious peg takes its place.

A peg may only jump over one peg at a time, and may not jump over an opponent's peg.

A peg may be moved along one of the lines to an immediately adjacent vacant peg hole if a capturing 'jump' is not possible.

CONSTRUCTION

Game board 12mm (½in) birch plywood
115mm (4¹⁷⁄₃₂in) × 115mm (4¹⁷⁄₃₂in).
Edging 21mm (1³⁄₁₆in) × 5mm (⁷⁄₃₂in) ramin
strip.
Peg holes 6mm (¼in) drilled at each
intersection of the playing grid.
Pegs Sixteen 30mm (1³⁄₁₆in) × 6mm (¼in) pegs.

MARKING AND FINISHING

The playing area of the game board is a grid of
25mm (1in) squares. This grid is 20mm (²⁵⁄₃₂in) in
from the edge all round.

The game board is left natural and varnished.

The edging is painted black and varnished.

Eight of the pegs are stained dark, and eight left
natural.

Fig 8.1
Four Field Kono game board.

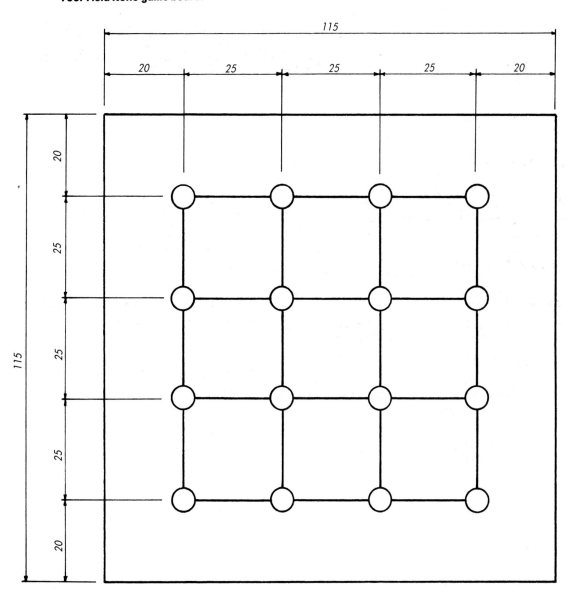

41

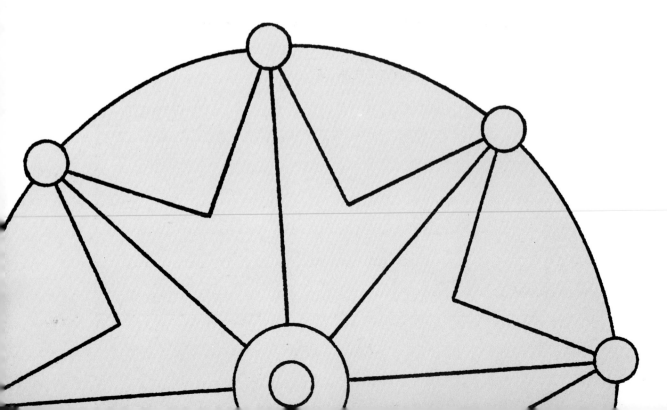

MU-TORERE

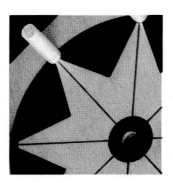

INTRODUCTION

Mu-Torere is believed to be the only board game of Maori origin — more active games are generally favoured. There is some dispute regarding the game's date of origin: some believe that it is of pure Maori origin, dating back prior to the arrival of Europeans in New Zealand, while others suggest that the name 'Mu' is derived from the English 'move' and that the game was adapted from draughts or checkers (*see* Fig 9.1). Whatever its origin, Mu-Torere is an enjoyable and challenging game.

OBJECT OF THE GAME

To block your opponent's pegs so that he is unable to move.

FOR TWO PLAYERS

EQUIPMENT

- Mu-Torere game board
- Four dark pegs and four light pegs

PREPARATION

Each player places his pegs in adjacent holes at the star points. The central, 'putahi', hole remains vacant.

PLAY

The dark pegs always begin, with the players then taking alternate turns. The players change colour at the end of each game.

There are three types of move:

1 A peg can be moved from a point to the putahi, providing that an opponent's peg occupies one, or both, adjacent points.
2 A peg can be moved from the putahi to any vacant point.
3 A peg can be moved from one point to an unoccupied, adjacent point.

Pegs are not allowed to jump over other pegs.

CONSTRUCTION

Game board 12mm (½in) birch plywood 110mm (4⁵⁄₁₆in) × 110mm (4⁵⁄₁₆in).
Edging 21mm (1³⁄₁₆in) × 6mm (¼in) ramin strip.
Peg holes 6mm (¼in) diameter — there are nine holes in total: one in the centre of the board, and one at each outer point of the star.
Pegs Eight 30mm (1³⁄₁₆in) × 6mm (¼in) pegs.

MARKING AND FINISHING

Plot the outer circle from the centre of the board, using a compass; the diameter is 90mm (3 $^{17}/_{32}$in).

Plot a second circle with a diameter of 50mm (2in).

Measure 45° lines from the centre. The points at which these lines cross the outer circle mark the outer points of the star.

The inner star points are located by drawing lines from the centre, halfway between the 45° lines (22.5°). The points at which these lines cross the inner circle mark the inner star points.

Pencil the lines from the star outer points to the inner ones.

Pen all the relevant circles and lines, and erase any construction lines. French curves may be helpful when penning in the outer circle.

Varnish the board and paint in the black areas before applying the final coats of varnish.

The edging is painted black and varnished.

Four pegs are stained a dark brown and four left natural.

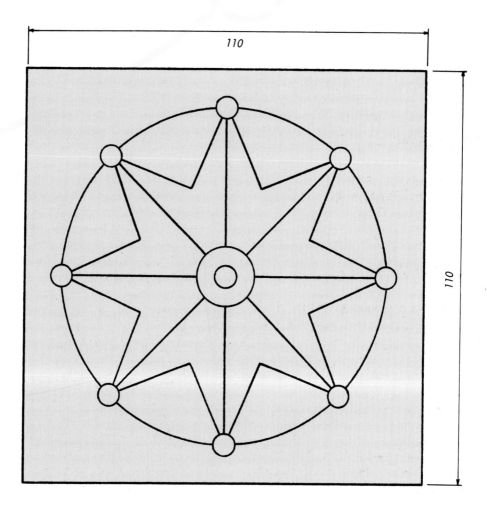

Fig 9.1
Mu-Torere game board.

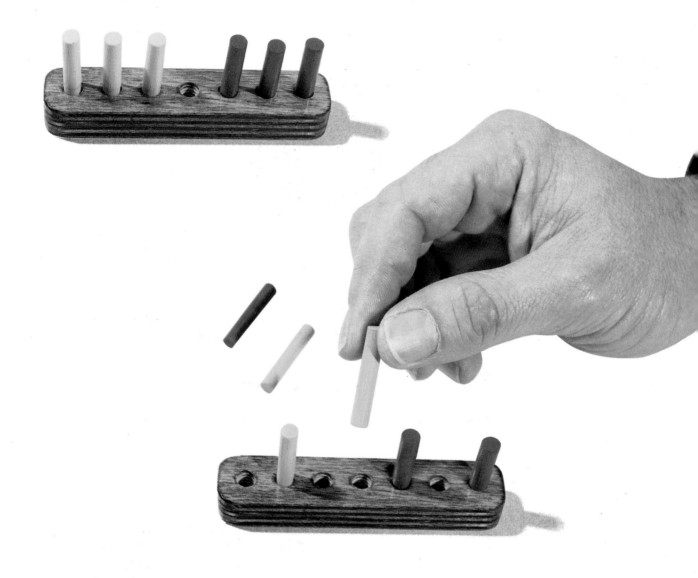

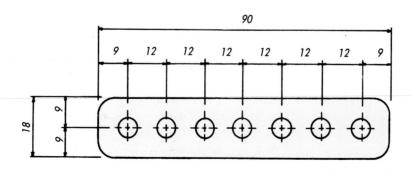

Fig 10.1
All Change game board.

10

ALL CHANGE

INTRODUCTION

This pocket-sized game is ideal for whiling away a few spare minutes in the day — but it is not as simple as it looks!

OBJECT OF THE GAME

To change the places of the two sets of pegs in 15 moves or less.

FOR ONE PLAYER

PLAY

A peg may make the following moves:

- Move forward one hole when the hole ahead is vacant.
- Jump over another peg when the hole beyond is vacant.

The pegs may only move forwards, never backwards.

CONSTRUCTION

Game board 12mm (1/2in) birch plywood 90mm (3^{17}/$_{32}$in) × 18mm (3/4in), with the corner edges rounded to a 10mm (3/8in) radius.

Peg holes Seven 6mm (1/4in) peg holes are drilled an equal distance apart down the centre of the game board.

Pegs Six 6mm (1/4in) × 30mm (1^3/$_{16}$in) pegs.

MARKING AND FINISHING

The board was stained with Indian rosewood wood dye and varnished.

Three of the pegs are coloured red, and three yellow.

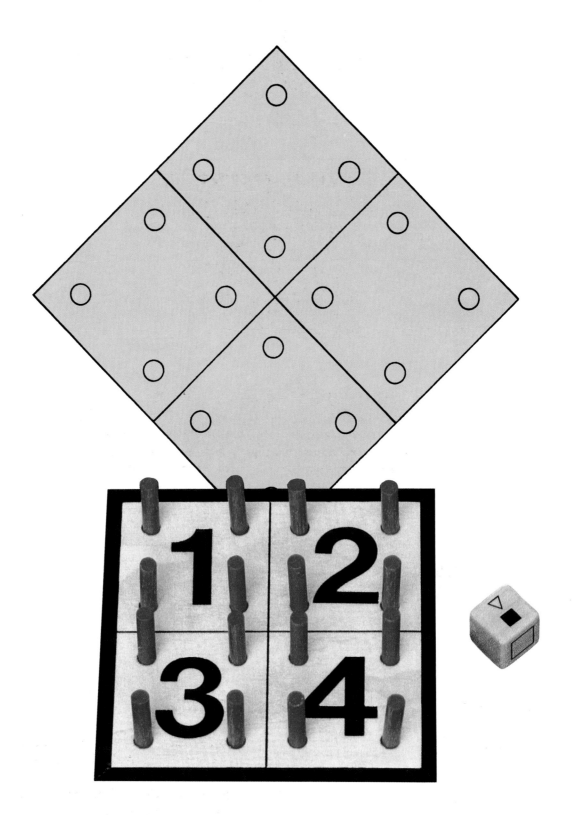

11
PINCH IT!

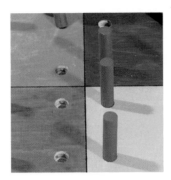

INTRODUCTION

This game enables the players to find out who their friends really are! By rolling the specially marked die, players are instructed to remove their own pegs or pinch one of their opponent's pegs — whose will you pinch?

OBJECT OF THE GAME

To be the last player left in the game with one or more pegs in your possession.

FOR TWO TO FOUR PLAYERS

EQUIPMENT

● Pinch It! game board
● 16 pegs
● Die

PREPARATION

Each player has one square section of the board, and places four pegs into the holes provided.

Determine which player will start the game. Play moves in a clockwise direction.

PLAY

Each player rolls the die once in turn, and acts upon the roll as follows:

Blank no action is taken, and play passes to the next player.

☐ the player making the die roll must remove one of his own pegs from the board and discard it. All discarded pegs should be kept near the board, as they may be required later in the game.

▷ the player making the die roll may take a peg from any player of his choice, and discard it.

■ the player making the die roll may take a discarded peg (if any) and place it into one of his own vacant peg holes. If no peg holes are available, he cannot act upon the die roll, and play moves on to the next player.

■ △ the player making the die roll may take a peg from any player of his choice and place it in a vacant peg hole of his own. If no peg hole is available, the peg is discarded.

If a player loses all his pegs, he is out of the game. The winner of the game is the player who is the only one left with a peg or pegs in play.

CONSTRUCTION

Game board 12mm (½in) birch plywood 100mm (4in) × 100mm (4in), for both game board designs.

Edging 17mm (¹¹⁄₁₆in) × 5mm (⁷⁄₃₂in) ramin strip for the numbered board. 21mm (¹³⁄₁₆in) × 5mm (⁷⁄₃₂in) ramin strip for the coloured board.

Peg holes 6mm (¼in) diameter. Each board is divided in four equal sections, each section having four peg holes drilled into it.

Pegs Sixteen 30mm (1³⁄₁₆in) × 6mm (¼in) dowel pegs are required for each game board.

Dice One 18mm (¾in) die for each game board.

MARKING AND FINISHING

The coloured board: the colours shown in the photograph on p. 50 are stains made from thinned artist's acrylic blue, yellow, green and orange. The edging and pegs are left natural.

Fig 11.1
Pinch It! game board.

The numbered board: this is numbered using 30mm (1³⁄₁₆in) sticky-back numbers used for signs and labelling. The edging is painted black and the pegs are stained red.

The die is marked as follows:

□

▷

■

■ △

Two **blank** sides

ALTERNATIVES

A game board constructed with a 'well' in the centre, for storing the discarded pegs in during play, would be useful.

More sections could be added to a board, to enable a greater number of players to participate.

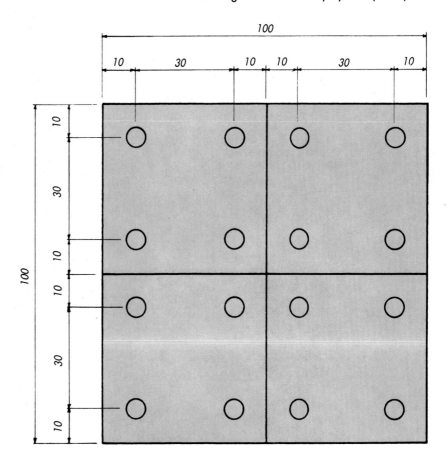

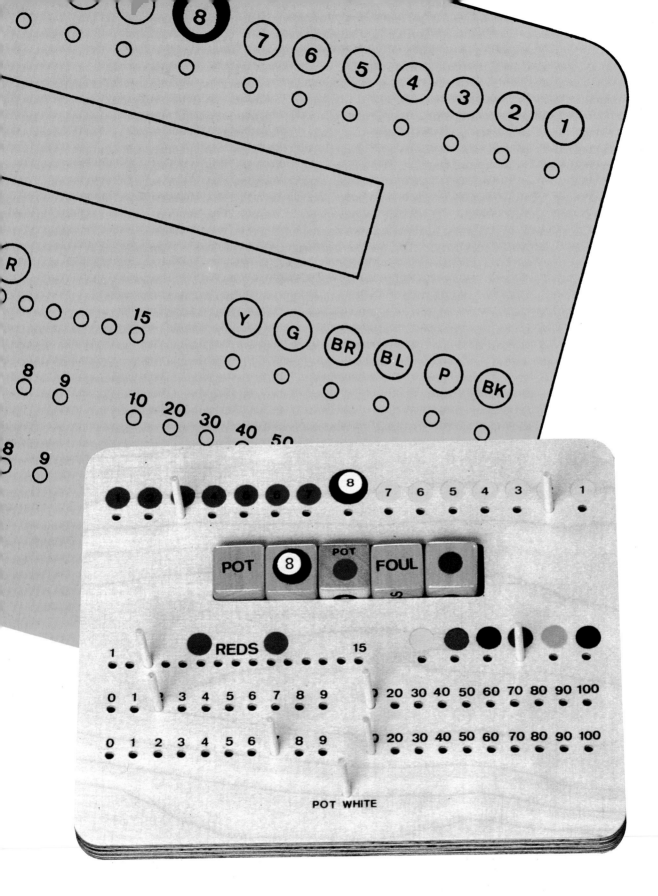

12

POOL, BILLIARDS AND SNOOKER DICE

INTRODUCTION

All the basic elements of pool, billiards and snooker are incorporated in these dice games. Ideal for carrying around, these dice versions allow you to play the games almost anywhere, without the need for a large space or expensive equipment (*see* Fig 12.1).

The scoreboard is not essential, as scoring may be kept with pen and paper. The dice can be made for individual games only.

ALL THE GAMES ARE FOR TWO PLAYERS

SCOREBOARD CONSTRUCTION

Scoreboard 12mm (½in) birch plywood 184mm (7¼in) × 148mm (5¹³⁄₁₆in), plus a piece of 3mm (⅛in) hardboard of equal size. The birch plywood forms the top of the scoreboard, and the hardboard the backing. After the dice holder has been cut and all the peg holes have been drilled into the birch plywood, the hardboard backing is glued into place and trimmed. Once the glue has set, all four corners of the scoreboard are rounded off.
Peg holes All the peg holes are 3mm (⅛in) diameter.
Dice holder The rectangular slot used for storing the dice is cut out using a fretsaw.

Pegs Eight 3mm (⅛in) × 30mm (1³⁄₁₆in) pegs, used as score markers.

SCOREBOARD MARKING AND FINISHING

The balls are marked by painting self-adhesive labels and applying them to the scoreboard.

The letters and numbers are 4mm (⁵⁄₃₂in) and 2.5mm (³⁄₃₂in) transfers.

The scoreboard is left natural and varnished.

The scoring pegs are left natural.

POOL DICE

OBJECT OF THE GAME

To successfully pot all seven of your own pool balls and then
the 8-ball before your opponent, without prematurely
potting the 8-ball.

EQUIPMENT

- One Pot Die marked:
  POT, POT, POT, FOUL, MISS, MISS
- One Foul Die marked:
  x2, x2, x2, x2, 0Bx2, 8
- Scoreboard or pencil and paper

PREPARATION

Determine which player will start the
game.

PLAY

At the start of play each player has seven balls of
his own to pot. To win the game, a player must
successfully pot these seven balls followed by the
8-ball. The 8-ball must not be potted out of turn –
the penalty for doing so is to lose the game.

POT DIE

The first player rolls the Pot Die:

If **POT** is rolled, he has successfully potted a ball.
He then re-rolls the die.

If **FOUL** is rolled, he has made a foul shot. That
player's turn has now come to an end, and he
must roll the Foul Die to determine his penalty.

If **MISS** is rolled, the ball has not been potted and
the player's turn has finished.

FOUL DIE

When a player has committed a foul (rolled
FOUL on the Pot Die), he must roll the Foul Die to
determine the penalty he has incurred.

If **x2** is rolled, the opposing player is awarded an
extra shot. This means that if during his turn he
rolls **MISS**, he is allowed to roll the Pot Die again
and his turn does not end. Only one extra shot is
allowed per ×2. If the opposing player rolls
FOUL, he may not take an extra turn, but must
end his turn and himself roll the Foul Die to
determine his penalty.

If **0Bx2** is rolled, this means that one of the
opponent's balls has been potted by mistake, and
an extra shot is awarded to the opponent in his
next turn. The potting player's turn is now over.

If **8** is rolled, the black 8-ball has been mistakenly
potted. The game ends here, with the player who
potted the 8-ball losing the game.

Note: if a player is attempting to pot the 8-ball
and rolls a **FOUL** followed by **8** on the Foul Die,
he does not lose the game but takes the ×2
penalty. Also, if both players only need to pot the
8-ball and one rolls **0Bx2** (opponent's ball is
potted by mistake), he must take the ×2 penalty.

SCORING

At the top of the scoreboard there is an 8-ball
symbol, with seven red balls to its left and seven
yellow balls to its right. Each set of red and yellow
balls is numbered 1–7. Before the game begins,
decide which player is to pot the red balls and
who is to pot the yellow balls.

Underneath the numbered balls are peg holes.
Place a peg into the hole beneath the number '1'
ball when the first ball of a set is potted. Move the
peg along as further balls are potted.

If you do not wish to use the scoreboard, the score
can be kept using pencil and paper. Reproduce
the appropriate part of the scoreboard by

drawing it on to paper (*see* Fig 12.2). One player is allotted the balls on the left, and the other the balls on the right. Strike off a ball that has been potted with a pencil.

CONSTRUCTION

Dice Two 18mm (¾in) dice.

POOL DICE MARKING AND FINISHING

The two dice are left natural.

The Pot Die is marked using 4mm (⁵/₃₂in) black transfer letters as follows:

POT, POT, POT, FOUL, MISS, MISS

The Foul Die is marked as follows:

x2, x2, x2, x2, 0Bx2, 8

The 8-ball symbol consists of a black-painted 12mm (½in) self-adhesive paper label with a smaller 8mm (⁵/₁₆in) white label stuck on to it. A 4mm (⁵/₃₂in) number 8 is applied to the white label.

All the other symbols are 4mm (⁵/₃₂in) black transfers.

Both dice are varnished after the markings have been applied.

Fig 12.1
Pool, Billiards and Snooker Dice scoreboard.

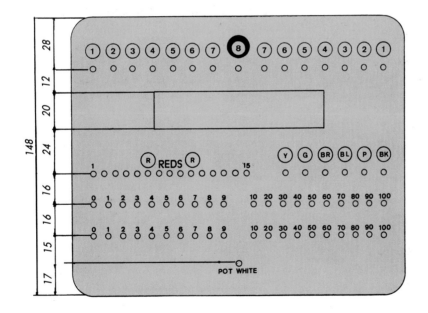

R ....RED
Y ....YELLOW
G ....GREEN
BR ...BROWN
BL ...BLUE
P ....PINK
BK ...BLACK

Fig 12.2
Alternative Pool Dice scoreboard.

55

BILLIARDS DICE

OBJECT OF THE GAME

To be the first player to reach a predetermined score, e.g. 50, 100 or 150 points. The first to do so is the winner.

EQUIPMENT

- One Billiard Die marked **C, POT WHITE, POT RED, OFF WHITE, OFF RED, NO SCORE**
- Scoreboard or pencil and paper

PREPARATION

Determine which player begins the game and what the target score is to be.

PLAY

The starting player rolls the die.

If **C** (Cannon) is rolled, the player's cue ball has struck both the other balls on the table. **Score 2 points.**

If **OFF WHITE** is rolled, the player's cue ball has gone into a pocket after hitting the white ball. **Score 2 points.**

If **OFF RED** is rolled, the player's cue ball has gone into a pocket after hitting the red ball. **Score 3 points.**

If **POT RED** is rolled, the red ball has been potted. **Score 3 points.**

If **POT WHITE** is rolled, the white ball has been potted. **Score 2 points.**

When POT WHITE is rolled, the white ball, as in the real game, is not re-spotted, i.e. it may not be re-rolled in that players turn, or 'break'. If it is, the player's break is over and play passes to his opponent. When the white ball is potted, place a peg into the 'Pot White' peg hole on the scoreboard.

Play alternates between players, changing at the end of each break. The first player to reach the predetermined total number of points is the winner.

SCORING

The score can be kept on the bottom two rows of peg holes on the scoreboard. One player has the top row, and the other the bottom row. Remove the pegs and score as the balls are potted. Units of tens are on the right, single units on the left.

The score may also be kept with pencil and paper.

Player A	Player B
2	2*
3	3
2	2
2*	EB 7
3	

Note: * denotes white ball is potted.
EB = end of break

In the example above, Player B has started play. His turn ended on the score of 7. Player A is still playing, but he has potted the white ball, so his turn may end soon.

0 1 2 3 4 5 6 8 9 0 20 30 40 50 60 70 80 90 100

POT WHITE

56

CONSTRUCTION

Dice One 18mm (¾in) die.

BILLIARDS DICE MARKING AND FINISHING

The die is left natural and marked with the following:

C (Cannon) 10mm (⅜in) black transfer letters.

POT WHITE POT is 2.5mm (³⁄₃₂in) black transfer letters; WHITE is an 8mm (³⁄₁₆in) round self-adhesive label painted white.

POT RED as POT WHITE — except that it is red!

OFF WHITE as POT WHITE, except OFF is substituted for POT.

OFF RED as POT RED, except OFF is substituted for POT.

NO SCORE 2.5mm (³⁄₃₂in) black transfer letters.

The die is varnished once the markings have been applied.

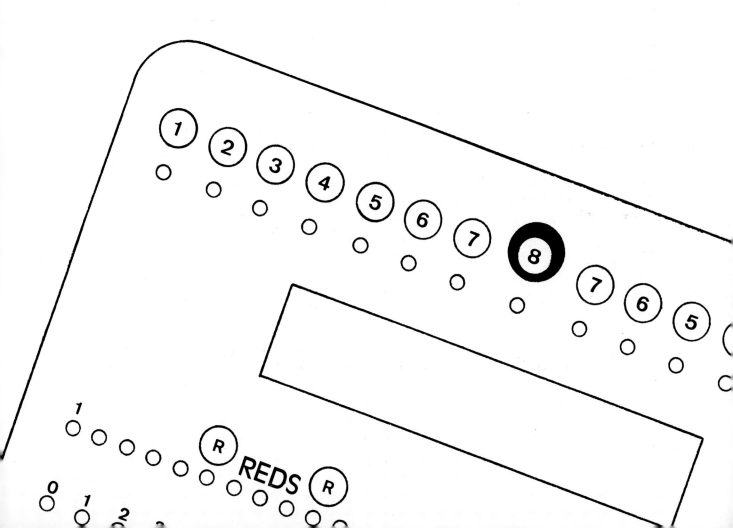

SNOOKER DICE

OBJECT OF THE GAME

To score more points than your opponent by, for the most part, potting the most snooker balls. As in the actual game of snooker, the players must between them pot all the 15 red balls and then the colours in sequence. After every red ball is potted, a colour must be attempted. If the colour is successfully potted, it is deemed re-spotted until all the reds have been potted.

EQUIPMENT

- One Pot Die marked **POT, POT, POT, POT, FOUL, MISS**
- One Coloured Ball Die marked **YELLOW, GREEN, BROWN, BLUE, PINK, BLACK**
- Scoreboard or pencil and paper

PREPARATION

Determine which player will start the game.

PLAY

The game begins with the first player rolling the Pot Die:

If **POT** is rolled, a red ball has been potted. **Score 1 point.** The player must now roll the die again to see if he can pot a coloured ball. If POT is rolled again, the attempt has been successful. The player now rolls the Coloured Ball Die to determine which colour was potted, and scores as follows:

Yellow	**2 points**
Green	**3 points**
Brown	**4 points**
Blue	**5 points**
Pink	**6 points**
Black	**7 points**

If **FOUL** is rolled, this means that a foul shot has been committed. The Coloured Ball Die is rolled to determine the penalty score, which is added to the opponent's score:

Yellow	**4 points**
Green	**4 points**
Brown	**4 points**
Blue	**5 points**
Pink	**6 points**
Black	**7 points**

If **MISS** is rolled, this means that the player has been unable to pot a ball, and his turn ends.

SCORING

The position of play in the game (on the snooker table) is shown by using the row of peg holes immediately below the dice holder.

When a red ball is potted, place a peg in the relevant peg hole. Move the peg along (from the hole marked 1 to the hole marked 15) as the red balls are potted. After all 15 have been potted, move the peg on to the colour section to the right.

The scores of the individual players are kept using the bottom two rows of peg holes. One player uses the upper row, one the lower row.

If you do not use the scoreboard, the score can be kept using pencil and paper. Copy the red and coloured ball lines from the scoreboard on to a piece of paper. As each ball is potted, a line is put through it. To keep the individual scores, keep a running total recorded on paper.

CONSTRUCTION

Dice Two 18mm ($\frac{3}{4}$in) dice.

SNOOKER DICE MARKING AND FINISHING

Both dice are left natural.

The Pot Die is lettered with 4mm ($\frac{5}{32}$in) transfers as follows:

POT, POT, POT, POT, FOUL, MISS

The Coloured Ball Die is marked with six different coloured balls, one per side. These are made of 8mm ($\frac{5}{16}$in) self-adhesive labels painted the relevant colours using modeller's enamel paint. The colours are:

yellow, green, brown, blue, pink, black

Both dice are varnished after the markings have been applied.

13

CRICKET DICE

INTRODUCTION

This simple-to-play game allows you to play cricket almost anywhere — car, train, plane, pub, club or at home! The dice replace bat and ball, and the score is kept on paper.

OBJECT OF THE GAME

To be the team which has scored the highest number of runs at the end of the game.

FOR TWO PLAYERS

EQUIPMENT

- One Batting Die marked
  0, 1, 2, 4, 6, ?
- One Fielding Die
  NOT OUT, NOT OUT, LBW, C, B, S
- Pen and paper for scoring

PREPARATION

Determine the size of each team: as in the actual sport of cricket, each team could consist of eleven players, but for a shorter game six players per team is a good number. (Players in each team could be named after your favourite cricket players, or, for children, cartoon characters, etc.)

Draw up the score sheet using the players' names (or letters), ready to record the batting score.

Decide which team will bat first.

PLAY

The team batting first rolls the **Batting Die** for their first batsman. If a number is rolled, the batsman scores that number of runs. The die is rolled again, and the batsman's total is added to until ? is rolled.

This symbol represents the cry of **'owzat'** or, more grammatically, 'How was that?', meaning that the fielding side has appealed to the umpire to give the batsman out.

The player in control of the fielding team now rolls the **Fielding Die.**

If **NOT OUT** is rolled, the appeal has not been successful, and the batsman remains in and continues to bat.

If **LBW** (Leg Before Wicket)
If **C** (Caught)

If **B** (Bowled)

or **S** (Stumped) are rolled, the batsman is out.

The next batsman, if any are still to bat, now comes in to bat.

When the last batsman of the batting team is out, the fielding team becomes the batting team and vice versa.

SCORING

The score is kept with pen and paper. For example:

Name	Score	Total
Batsman **A**	2, 2, 0, 6, C	10
Batsman **B**	0, 4, 2, 1, 4, LBW	11
Batsman **C**	1, S	1
Batsman **D**	6, 1, 2, 6, 0, 1, 4, 4, 2, C	26
Batsman **E**	B	0
Batsman **F**	1, 0, 0, 4, 1, 6, 2, 2, B	16
	TOTAL TEAM SCORE	**64**

CONSTRUCTION

Dice Two 18mm (¾in) dice.

MARKING AND FINISHING

The Batting Die is marked with the following 8mm (⁵⁄₁₆in) black transfers:

0, 1, 2, 4, 6, ? (The Batting Die has four small **?**s, but one 8mm (⁵⁄₁₆in) would suffice.)

The Fielding Die is marked with the following black transfers:

NOT OUT, NOT OUT, LBW – all 4mm (⁵⁄₃₂in) **B, S, C** – all 12mm (½in)

Both dice are left natural and varnished.

14

WORD DICE

INTRODUCTION

Word games enjoy great popularity today. They provide a mental challenge which can be enjoyed as solo or group games, and by young and old alike.

Word Dice can be played in two separate ways; both versions of the game are equally stimulating and brain-teasing.

OBJECT OF THE GAME

Version One
To be the first player to score a predetermined total number of points (i.e. 100 or 200). Points are gained by constructing as many words as possible using the random letters shown from a roll of the eight dice.

Version Two
To be the first player to score a predetermined total number of points. Players must try to make one or two words (no more), using the random letters shown from a roll of the eight dice.

FOR ANY NUMBER OF PLAYERS

EQUIPMENT

- Eight dice marked with the appropriate letters
- Paper and pens
- Watch or clock with second hand
- Dictionary

PLAY: VERSION ONE

The game is divided into a series of rounds. Each round is timed, and lasts one minute.

Players take it in turns to time each round and to roll the dice.

A player rolls all eight dice simultaneously. Once the dice have stopped rolling, the round begins.

During the minute the players make as many words of three letters or more as they can out of the letters shown.

Letters may only be used once in any one word, but can be used again to construct separate words. If a blank is rolled, any letter may be used for that die; the letter may change from word to word. Pronouns and plurals are not allowed.

Players write their words down on to a piece of paper. At the end of each round, the score of each correct word is calculated, totalled up, and added to the players' running totals.

SCORING – VERSION ONE

Points are awarded as follows:

3-letter word – **3** points
4-letter word – **4** points
5-letter word – **5** points
6-letter word – **6** points
7-letter word – **8** points
8-letter word – **12** points

PLAY: VERSION TWO

This version is also divided into one-minute rounds; the difference from Version One is the way in which the letters on the dice are used.

Each letter (or blank) may be used only once, with the aim being to utilize as many dice as possible. For example:

Letters rolled = **T, blank, S, U, R, blank, O, M**

An eight-letter word MOISTURE can be constructed, with I and E being used for the blanks; or a five- and a three-letter word can be constructed: ATOMS and RUE, with A and E used for the blanks; or two four-letter words SUIT and ROOM, with I and O used for the blanks, can be constructed.

As in Version One, pronouns are not acceptable, but plurals can be used.

SCORING – VERSION TWO

Points are awarded as follows:

One **2**-letter word	**2** points
One **3**-letter word	**3** points
One **4**-letter word	**4** points
One **5**-letter word	**5** points
One **6**-letter word	**8** points
One **7**-letter word	**10** points
4- and **4**-letter words	**16** points
5- and **3**-letter words	**16** points
6- and **2**-letter words	**16** points
One **8**-letter word	**24** points

VERIFICATION OF WORDS

Before play, all players must agree upon a dictionary to be referred to if the spelling or the validity of a word is in doubt. Only words found in that dictionary will be deemed valid.

CONSTRUCTION

Dice Eight 18mm (¾in) dice.

MARKING AND FINISHING

The eight dice are marked with 10mm (⅜in) black
letter transfers as follows:

> Die **1** – M, S, B, H, Y, D
> Die **2** – X, J, Z, C, M, blank
> Die **3** – K, P, G, R, D, blank
> Die **4** – T, C, N, L, R, G
> Die **5** – S, F, B, W, Q, H
> Die **6** – Y, L, V, N, T, blank
> Die **7** – A, E, E, I, O, U
> Die **8** – A, E, E, I, O, U

To ensure clear identification of each letter, it is
useful to apply a line beneath certain letters to
indicate which way round they should be viewed
– i.e. N could be mistaken for a Z if viewed from
the side, so it should be marked N̲.

The dice are left natural and varnished.

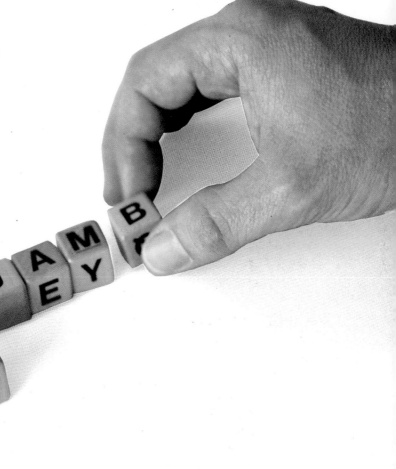

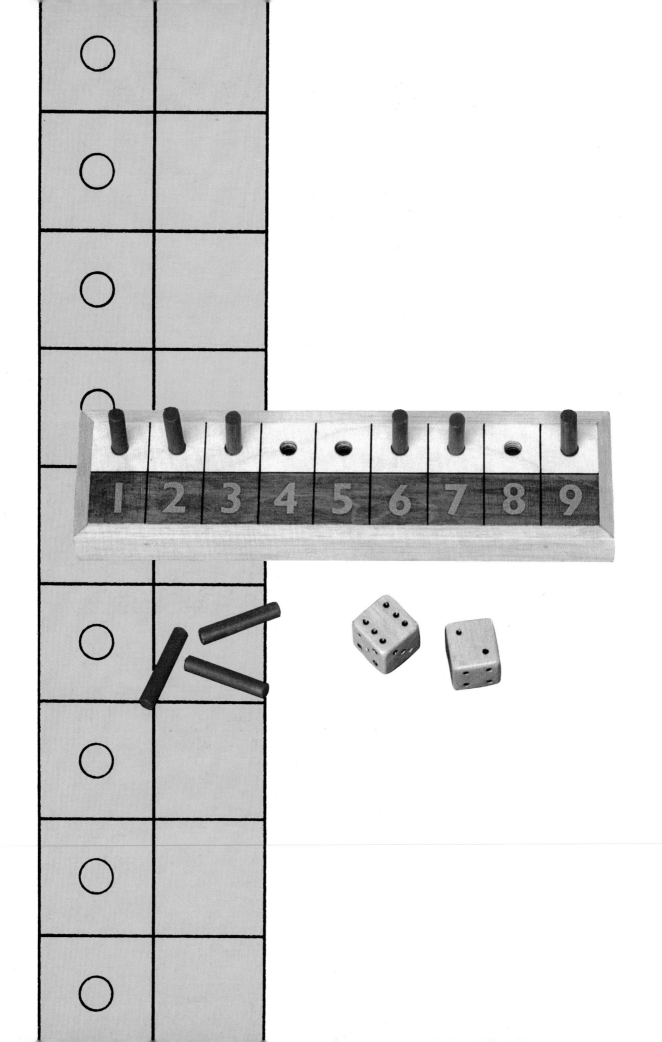

¹⁵ SHUT THE BOX

INTRODUCTION

Shut the Box has enjoyed popularity along the coastal regions of Northern France for about 200 years. Sailors and fishermen brought it over the Channel to Britain, where it is now played in pubs and clubs. Versions are also found in Central Africa. It is a competitive game, can be played as a patience game by one person, and is often played for stakes.

Shut the Box is usually played with equipment consisting of a tray in which to roll the dice, and nine numbered boxes with sliding lids. The game shown in Fig 15.1 has been simplified by using pegs instead of boxes and lids. The tray has also been omitted.

OBJECT OF THE GAME

Each player rolls the dice and tries to 'cover' or 'peg out' as many boxes as possible, aiming to end his turn with the lowest score for the round or game.

FOR ANY NUMBER OF PLAYERS

EQUIPMENT

● Shut the Box game board and nine pegs
● Two dice, each marked **1, 2, 3, 4, 5, 6**

PLAY

At the beginning of play all the pegs are removed from the game board.

One player begins the game and rolls both dice.

He may choose to use the two individual scores rolled, or the sum of the two, to 'peg out' a box or boxes. For example, if 5 and 2 are rolled, the player may place a peg in boxes 5 and 2, or box 7.

When the boxes 7, 8 and 9 have been pegged, only one die is rolled.

A turn ends when the player is unable to 'peg out' a box. The numbers of any remaining unpegged boxes are added together, and the total becomes that player's score.

After all the players have had their turn, the player with the lowest score wins the round or game.

A variation may be played, in which players are deemed out of the game when their score reaches 45. The last player left in the game wins.

In the patience version, the player tries to 'peg out' all the boxes in the lowest number of dice rolls possible.

CONSTRUCTION

Game board 12mm (½in) birch plywood 180mm (7³⁄₃₂in) × 40mm (1⁹⁄₁₆in).

Edging 17mm (1¹⁄₁₆in) × 5mm (⁷⁄₃₂in) ramin strip.

Peg holes 6mm (¼in) diameter, drilled into the centre of the top row of nine squares.

Pegs Nine 30mm (1³⁄₁₆in) × 6mm (¼in) dowel pegs.

Dice Two 18mm (¾in) dice.

MARKING AND FINISHING

The game board is divided into eighteen 20mm (²⁵⁄₃₂in) × 20mm (²⁵⁄₃₂in) sections.

The bottom row of nine squares is stained green. The numbers 1 to 9, placed in these squares, are 12mm (½in) gold transfers.

The top row of nine squares is left natural, along with the edging. The entire game board is varnished. The pegs are stained red.

The dice may be any colour, and should both be marked **1, 2, 3, 4, 5, 6.**

Fig 15.1
Shut the Box game board.

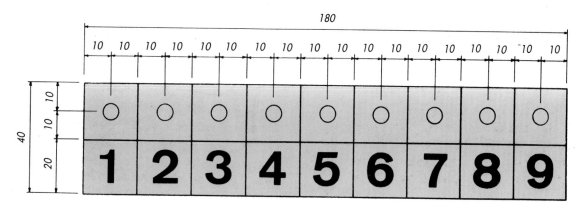

71

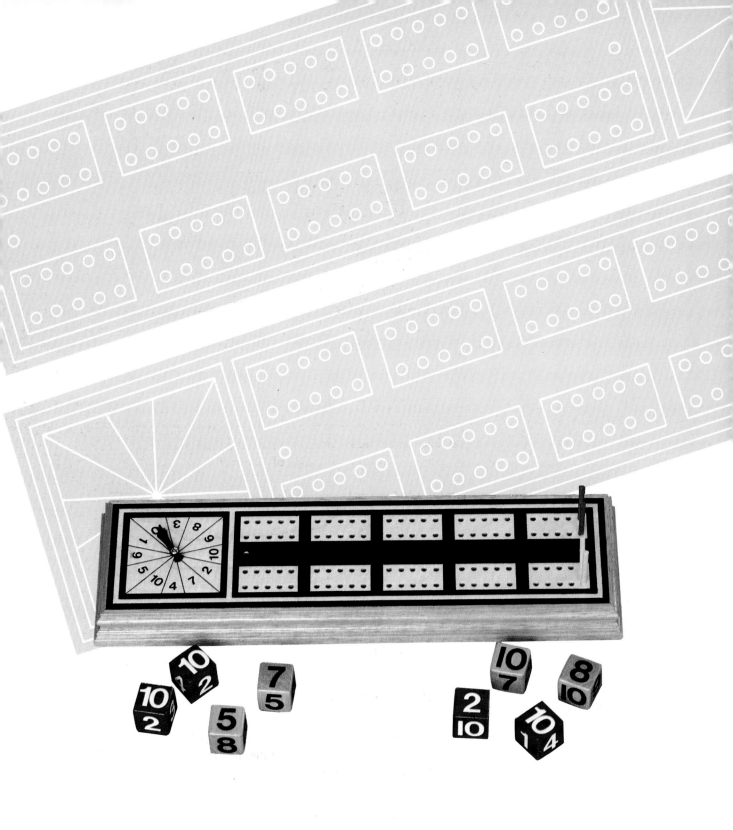

CRIBBAGE DICE

INTRODUCTION

Cribbage Dice relies upon the successful throws of the dice in order to gain scoring combinations of numbers.

Following similar rules to the card game of Cribbage, Cribbage Dice is primarily based on luck. It is more straightforward than the card game version, and provides an ideal introduction to the game for children; it is also an excellent game for developing counting skills.

Fortunes change rapidly in this variation of the enormously popular card game. No previous knowledge or experience of the card game of Cribbage is necessary in order to play Cribbage Dice.

OBJECT OF THE GAME

To be the first player to reach a previously agreed total number of points — 51, 101, or 151 — based on rolls of the dice to gain scoring combinations of numbers.

FOR TWO PLAYERS

73

EQUIPMENT

- Scoreboard including number spinner
- Eight dice – four dice for each player, two of each marked

    Die A (red) **1, 2, 3, 4, 10, 10**
    Die B (natural) **5, 6, 7, 8, 9, 10**

PLAY

Each round in the game of Cribbage Dice is divided into three sections: the **Play,** the **Show,** and the **Cribb.**

A spin of the spinner on the scoreboard is used to determine who holds the first Cribb – the lowest score wins.

THE PLAY

By alternate rolls of their four dice, the players aim to reach a cumulative total of exactly 31. Points may be scored after each roll of a die, dependent upon the number combination produced in conjunction with the dice roll or rolls immediately preceding it.

Scoring Combinations in the Play

Pair Two numbers the same .... **2** points
Threes Three numbers the same .... **6** points
Fours Four numbers the same .... **12** points
Fifteen When the cumulative total of the dice adds up to 15 .... **2** points

The non-Cribb holder commences the Play by selecting and rolling one of his four dice, announcing the number as it is rolled. The Cribb holder then selects and rolls a die similarly and announces the cumulative total of the two dice. Turns continue to alternate, each player announcing the cumulative value of the combined dice played to that stage, and also announcing any points scored with their rolls.

The cumulative total may not exceed 31. If a player's die roll takes the total beyond 31, he must take back the die and his go is finished. The last player to roll a die which adds to the cumulative score receives:

If the cumulative total is under 31 .... **1** point
If the cumulative total is exactly 31 .... **2** points

If either or both of the players have a die or dice left to roll, a second Play is started, following the alternate play rule, until all four of each player's dice have been rolled and counted.

The non-Cribb holder spins the pointer on the scoreboard before the Show and Cribb sections. The number indicated is the Spin Number for the rest of the round.

THE SHOW

Starting with the non-Cribb holder, each player in turn rolls all four of his dice. The Spin Number is now counted as a fifth dice roll for each player, and points are scored for combinations as in the Play (except for 31), with number sequences now also being awarded points as follows:

Three numbers in sequence .... **3** points
Four numbers in sequence .... **4** points

THE CRIBB

The player who holds the Cribb now has the opportunity of gaining extra points. Each player rolls one red and one natural die. The Spin Number is again added as a fifth dice roll, and points are awarded to the Cribb holder's score for scoring combinations, as for the Show.

The Cribb alternates between players, with the Play, Show and Cribb sections repeated until one player reaches the previously agreed total and wins the game.

SCORING

The score is kept on a specially designed Cribbage board, consisting of two rows of 25 small holes, split into groups of five for easy counting. Two additional holes, called the Game Holes, are positioned towards the middle of the board, one at each end. Each hole counts as one point.

Two pegs (or matchsticks) are used as markers for each player. The pegs travel up the length of the outer row of holes, towards the pointer, and back down the length of the inner holes, and, after completion of the appropriate number of lengths (agreed upon before the game has started), into the nearest game hole. The pegs are used as follows:

1 On the first score, one peg is moved the appropriate number of holes and left in the board as a marker.
2 On that player's second score, the other peg is advanced the appropriate number of holes beyond the first peg.
3 For the next and following scores, the peg showing the lowest score is moved the appropriate number of holes beyond the lead peg. The lead peg always indicates the score.

CONSTRUCTION

Scoreboard 12mm (½in) birch plywood 255mm (10¹⁄₁₆in) × 67mm (2⅝in).
Edging 21mm (¹³⁄₁₆in) base moulding.
Pointer 1.5mm (¹⁄₁₆in) birch plywood. The spinning pointer is cut out using a fretsaw (*see*

Fig 16.2), and is attached to the board by a small brass round head screw (suggested size No. 2 × ⅜in). A hole must be drilled through the pointer at the spot where the screw passes through; use the size of drill bit which will allow the pointer to spin freely but not too loosely.
Peg holes All 3mm (⅛in).
Pegs Four 3mm (⅛in) × 30mm (1³⁄₁₆in) pegs.
Dice Eight 18mm (¾in) dice.

MARKING AND FINISHING

Hobbyist enamel paint is used for the black areas on the scoreboard. The numbers are black 5mm (⁷⁄₃₂in) transfers.

Two scoring pegs are left natural, and two are stained red.

Four of the dice are coloured red and have white transfer numbers. Each is marked

1, 2, 3, 4, 10, 10

Four of the dice are left natural and have black transfer numbers. Each is marked

5, 6, 7, 8, 9, 10

The dice and the scoreboard are varnished.

Fig 16.2
Cribbage Dice scoreboard pointer.

Fig 16.1
Cribbage Dice scoreboard.

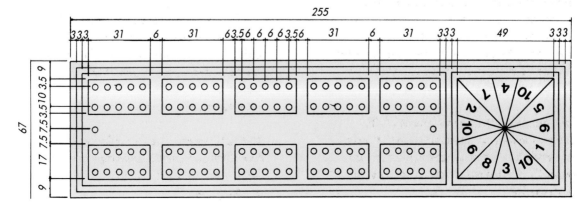

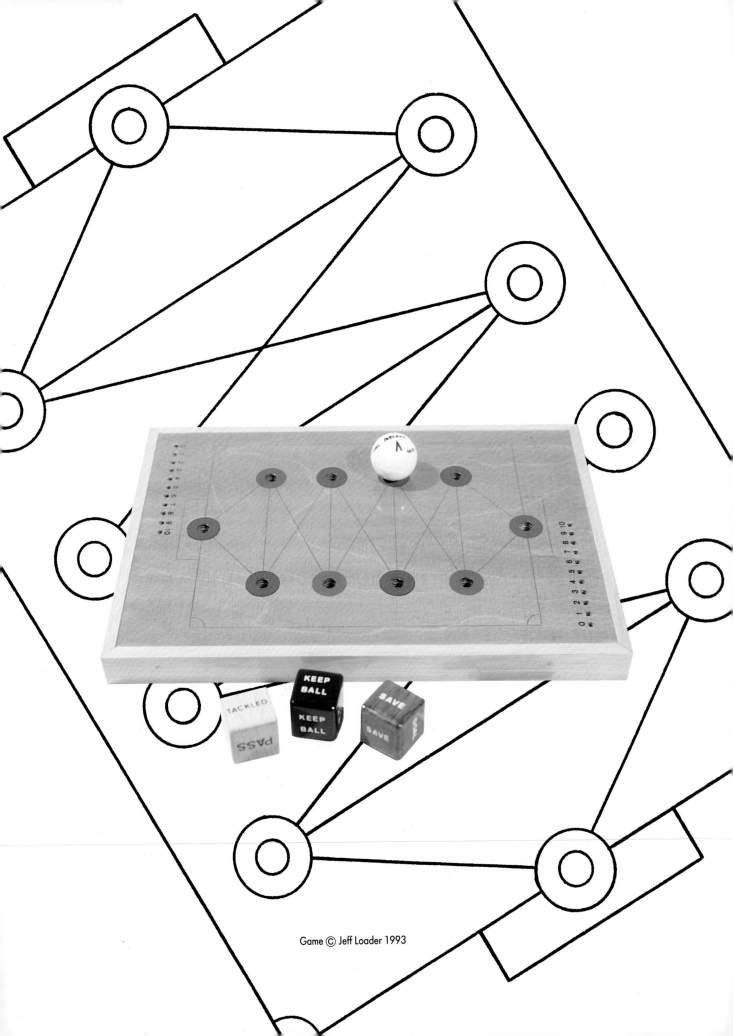

17

SOCCER

INTRODUCTION

Each player is in control of his own five-a-side soccer team. Using the special dice, the players build up attacks and try to score goals.

OBJECT OF THE GAME

To score more goals than your opponent in a given period of time.

FOR TWO PLAYERS

EQUIPMENT

- Soccer game board with ball and two scoring pegs
- One Passing Die marked **Pass, Pass, Pass, Pass, Tackled, Tackled**
- One Tackling Die marked **Keep Ball, Keep Ball, Keep Ball, Lose Ball, Lose Ball, Lose Ball**
- One Shooting Die marked **Save, Save, Save, Goal, Goal, Post**

PREPARATION

Place each team's scoring peg in the holes marked 0.

Determine which team will commence play.

Place the ball in the goalkeeper's position of the team which is to start play; the kickoff takes place from here.

PLAY

To score a goal, each team must pass the ball along the black lines, from footballer to footballer until the player closest to the opposing team's goal (the forward) has possession. When this is achieved, the forward may shoot for goal.

PASSING AND TACKLING

The goalkeeper kicks off and starts the game by rolling the Passing Die.

If **Pass** is rolled, the ball is moved, following the black lines, to the next footballer of his own team. The Passing Die is rolled again.

If **Tackled** is rolled, the player must roll the Tackling Die.

If **Keep Ball** is rolled, the player has beaten the tackle and kept possession of the ball. He continues play by rolling the Passing Die again.

If **Lose Ball** is rolled, the player has lost the tackle, and possession of the ball passes along a black line to the opposition's footballer, who is directly opposite. (If a forward loses the ball, it does not pass to the goalkeeper, but to the

opposition's footballer directly opposite the forward on the game board.) The other team, now in possession of the ball, roll the Passing Die and the game continues as described above.

If a goalkeeper in possession of the ball is successfully tackled, the ball passes to the opposition's forward, who immediately shoots for goal.

SHOOTING FOR GOAL

When the ball reaches the forward of a team, he shoots for goal by rolling the Shooting Die:

If **Save** is rolled, the shot has been saved by the goalkeeper. Possession of the ball passes to the opposition, and play begins again with the goalkeeper.

If **Goal** is rolled, a goal has been scored. The goal is recorded by moving the scoring peg to mark the appropriate number. Play recommences with a kickoff by the defending goalkeeper.

If **Post** is rolled, the ball has hit the post and rebounded back to the shooting forward, who may immediately shoot again.

78

CONSTRUCTION

Game board 12mm (½in) birch plywood 210mm (8⁹⁄₃₂in) × 140mm (5½in).
Edging 17mm (¹¹⁄₁₆in) × 5mm (⁷⁄₃₂in) ramin strip.
Peg holes Two lines of eleven 3mm (⅛in) diameter peg holes are required for scoring; the 10 soccer players' peg holes are 6mm (¼in) diameter.
Pegs Two 3mm (⅛in) pegs for scoring.
Ball A shop-bought model football is used for the ball. After drilling a 6mm (¼in) hole into it, a short piece of 6mm (¼in) dowel rod is glued into it: the dowel should protrude enough to allow it to be placed into the soccer players' peg holes — approximately 6mm (¼in)–10mm (⅜in). A wooden bead, 20mm (²⁵⁄₃₂in)–25mm (1in), could be substituted for the ball.
Dice Three 18mm (¾in) dice.

MARKING AND FINISHING

The pitch is coloured green (to represent grass): we used an acrylic green, thinned to a light tone and applied.

Painted 15mm (¹⁹⁄₃₂in) paper ring reinforcements (the type used to reinforce paper for ring binder folders) are stuck around the ten 6mm (¼in) peg holes to represent the soccer players. An alternative method would be to pen and colour a circle around each peg hole. Five are coloured blue, five red.

The lines of 3mm (⅛in) scoring peg holes are numbered using black 2.5mm (³⁄₃₂in) transfers.

The scoring pegs are left natural.

The dice are each given a different colour so as to be easily distinguishable. One is stained black, one mahogany, and one is left natural. They are marked with 2.5mm (³⁄₃₂in) transfers as follows, and then varnished.

Passing Die (natural) **Pass, Pass, Pass, Pass, Tackled, Tackled**

Tackling Die (black) **Keep Ball, Keep Ball, Keep Ball, Lose Ball, Lose Ball, Lose Ball**

Shooting Die (mahogany) **Save, Save, Save, Goal, Goal, Post**

Fig 17.1
Soccer game board.

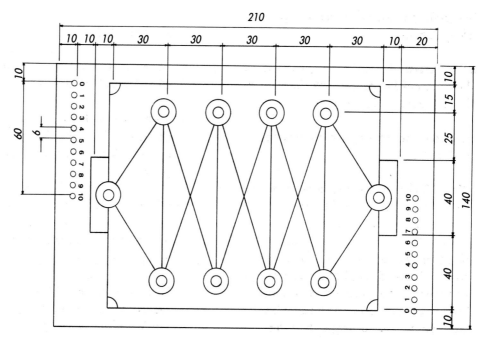

79

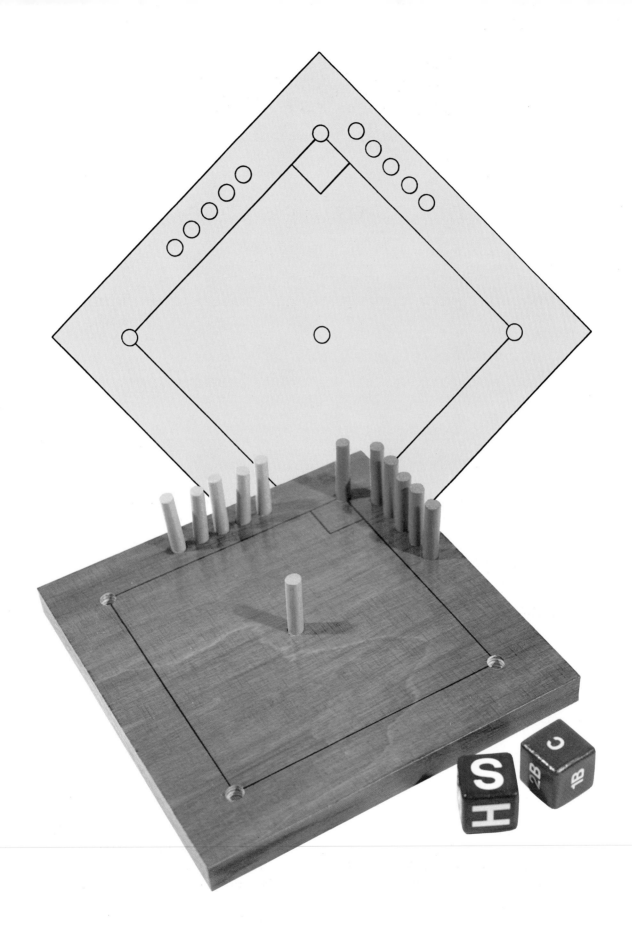

A Grand Slam occurs when the bases are loaded (when a batsman is on each base) and a HR (home run) is rolled on the die.

The score may be kept on a grid as shown in Fig 18.2: the numbers at the top represent each of the nine innings. The total score gained by each team during each innings is placed in the appropriate box. The total score of all the innings is added up and placed in the end 'Total' section.

The highest total score wins the game.

CONSTRUCTION

Game board 12mm (½in) birch plywood 140mm (5½in) × 140mm (5½in).
Peg holes All 6mm (¼in) in diameter.
Pegs Twelve 30mm (1³⁄₁₆in) × 6mm (¼in) dowel pegs.
Edging The game board is edged with wood effect self-adhesive plastic sheeting.
Dice Two 18mm (¾in) dice.

MARKING AND FINISHING

The game board is stained green and varnished.

Six of the pegs are coloured yellow, and six orange.

One die is coloured blue and lettered with the following transfers:

S, S, S, H, H, H

The other die is coloured red and lettered with the following transfers:

1B, 1B, 2B, C, C, HR

Fig 18.1
Baseball game board.

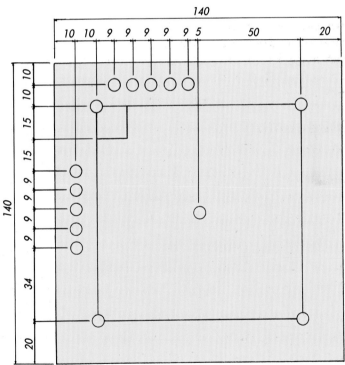

Fig 18.2
Baseball scoresheet.

TEAM	1	2	3	4	5	6	7	8	9	TOTAL

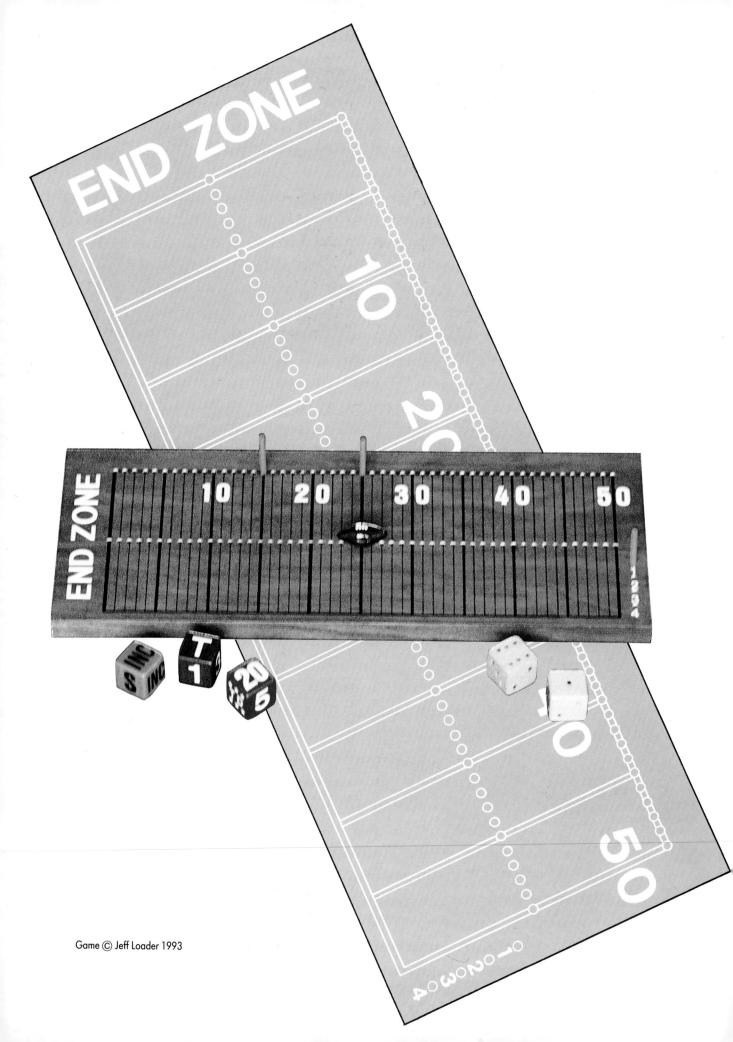

19

END ZONE

INTRODUCTION

In this tactical game each player takes on the role of coach for his own American Football team.

Each team has to move the ball from the 50-yard line to the End Zone in order to score points (*see* Fig 19.1). The coaches have to make the critical choice of which plays to use – pass, run, or attempt a field goal – to achieve this. Who has the greatest skill?

The playing pitch has been reduced from the actual 100 yards in the real game to 50 yards in the board game.

OBJECT OF THE GAME

To be the team coach who scores the highest number of points in a given period of time.

FOR TWO PLAYERS

EQUIPMENT

● End Zone game board with football and three pegs
● Two ordinary dice each marked 1, 2, 3, 4, 5, 6
● One Rushing die marked
    1 – amount of yards gained
    1 – amount of yards gained
    2 – amount of yards gained
    3 – amount of yards gained
    T – tackled
    T – tackled
● One Passing die marked
    C – complete
    C – complete
    INC – incomplete
    INC – incomplete
    INC – incomplete
    S – sacked

- One Completion die marked
    - **5** – amount of yards gained
    - **10** – amount of yards gained
    - **15** – amount of yards gained
    - **20** – amount of yards gained
    - **25** – amount of yards gained
    - **TD** – touchdown!

PREPARATION

The game time must be decided upon; 20–30 minutes is recommended.

Determine which team will start as the Offense and which the Defense.

Place the ball into the centre peg hole on the 50-yard line. Place one peg into the peg hole marked '1', one peg into the peg hole at the 50-yard line and one at the 40-yard line found at the edge of the playing pitch.

PLAY

To score points, the Offense team must try to move the ball towards the goal line – the End Zone. As in the real game, this is achieved using the 'Four Down System'.

FOUR DOWN SYSTEM

The Offense team has four attempts, called 'downs', in which to move the ball a minimum of 10 yards. Providing the minimum 10 yards have been gained within the four, or on the fourth down, play remains with that team and it is given another four downs in which to gain the minimum of another 10 yards. Play continues until the offense team either gains a touchdown or kicks a field goal.

The Offense team tries to gain as many yards as possible on each down, and on a successful down which takes it to the required minimum 10-yard line, will keep playing and gaining yardage beyond the 10-yard line until stopped by the Defense team.

If the Defense team only manages to stop the Offense team but does not gain possession of the ball, the next 10 yards required in four downs by the Offense team starts immediately from where the last play ended.

When the Offense team fails to gain 10 yards in four downs, it loses possession of the ball and the play. The other team changes from Defense to Offense.

Offense play also changes from one team to the other after a successful touchdown or field goal.

When Offense play changes from one team to the other, play always restarts at the 50-yard line.

GAINING YARDAGE

The Offense team may try to gain yardage by either:

Passing – carried out in the actual game by a player called a quarterback throwing the ball to a player called a receiver; or
Rushing – in the actual game a player, called a running back, running with the ball.

PASSING

When a player wishes to pass the ball, he rolls the Passing Die:

If Incomplete (INC) is rolled, this means that the quarterback's throw has failed to find a receiver to catch the ball. This results in the end of that particular down.

If Sacked (S) is rolled, this means that the quarterback has been tackled before he could release the ball. The player on the Defense team must roll one ordinary die. A score of 1, 2 or 3 means that the quarterback fumbled the ball and it was regained by the opposition; play possession now changes. A score of 4, 5 or 6 indicates that, although sacked, the quarterback retains the ball. That particular down is now over with no yardage gained, but play possession remains unchanged.

If Complete (C) is rolled, this means that the quarterback's throw has been caught by a receiver. The Completion Die is now rolled:

If a number is rolled, this will indicate how many yards were gained with that throw. Move the ball forward on the game board the relevant number of yards. That particular down is now over. If the yardage shown is greater than that left on the pitch from ball to End Zone, then a touchdown is scored. Play possession then changes.

If Touchdown (TD) is rolled, this indicates that the ball has been thrown all the way to, and caught inside, the End Zone. Points are then scored by the Offense team and play possession passes to the other team.

RUSHING

The Rushing Die is used when a player wishes his team to 'run' the ball in order to gain yardage.

The Offense team rolls the Rushing Die and moves the ball according to the number of yards shown. The team keeps doing this until Tackled (T) is rolled – this means that the running back has been tackled, no further yards are gained and that the down has come to an end. If Tackled is rolled first, no yards will be gained and the down is at an end.

When, on a Rushing play, the ball reaches the End Zone, a touchdown is scored.

FIELD GOALS

In the actual game of American Football, this is where a player tries to 'place kick' the ball between the goalposts. A field goal may be attempted on any down, but is usually attempted on the last (fourth) down. After a field goal attempt, whether succcessful or not, play possession changes to the other team.

A field goal may not be attempted when the ball is at or within the 9-yard line near the End Zone.

To attempt a field goal, roll two standard dice, and consult the chart below:

Distance from the End Zone	To be Successful
10 yards	Must roll 4 or more
11 – 20 yards	Must roll 5 or more
21 – 30 yards	Must roll 6 or more
31 – 40 yards	Must roll 8 or more
41 – 50 yards	Must roll 9 or more

EXTRA POINT

After a touchdown has been scored, the Offense team has the chance to 'kick' an extra point. This process is similar to the field goal, and is taken from the 9-yard line.

The Offense team rolls two standard dice; if the combined score is 4 or over, the kick has been successful.

SCORING

Touchdown	**6** points
Field goal	**3** points
Extra point	**1** point

YARDAGE DOWN MARKERS

To indicate the minimum 10 yards needed to be gained during the downs, two orange pegs are placed into the peg holes at the side of the playing pitch. These peg holes correspond with the peg holes which the ball uses in the centre of the pitch.

At the start of the game, and when Offense play changes from team to team, one peg is placed at the 50-yard line and one at the 40-yard line. The ball is moved forward the relevant number of peg holes as play progresses; when 10 yards or more are gained, and when the play is stopped but possession of the ball is unchanged, the pegs are moved to indicate the new 10 yards required. (*See* example of play below.)

DOWN MARKERS

Four peg holes marked 1, 2, 3, and 4 are placed at one end of the pitch, to keep a record of how many downs have been used. Place a peg in the hole marked 1 for the first down, and move it as further downs are played.

EXAMPLE OF A PLAY AND USE OF THE DOWN MARKERS

The ball is on the 50-yard line, the yardage down markers are on the 50-yard and 40-yard lines, and the down marker marks the first down in hole 1.

The Offense team chooses to Pass the ball:
Roll one – **INC**
First down is used and no yardage gained; the ball is not moved. The down marker is placed in hole 2.

Roll two – **C** and 20 yds
The ball is moved forward 20 yards, and the required 10 yards has been gained.

The yardage down markers are moved forward to mark the 30-yard line (where the ball is and where play starts) and the 20-yard line, showing the next 10 yards which need to be gained from the next four downs. The down marker is placed back in hole 1.

The Offense team now chooses to Rush the ball:

Roll one   – **2**   the ball is moved forward 2 yards
Roll two   – **3**   the ball is moved forward 3 yards
Roll three – **3**   the ball is moved forward 3 yards
Roll four – **1**   the ball is moved forward 1 yard
Roll five – **2**   the ball is moved forward 2 yards and the required minimum 10 yards have been gained in one down

Roll six – **T**   the running back is tackled; this down ends with 11 yards gained.

The yardage down markers are moved forward to mark the 19-yard line (where the ball is and where play starts) and the 9-yard line.

The Offense Team chooses to Pass the ball:

Roll one – **INC**
First down is used and no yardage gained. The down marker is placed in hole 2.

The Offense Team chooses to Rush the ball:

Roll two – **T**
Second down is used and no yardage gained. The down marker is placed in hole 3.

The Offense Team chooses to Pass the ball:

Roll three – **C** and 10 yds
The ball is moved forward 10 yards; the required minimum 10 yards have been gained.

The yardage down markers are moved forward to mark the 9-yard line (where the ball is and where play starts) and, because there are only 9 yards left to the End Zone, the other peg is placed on the End Zone line. The down marker is placed in hole 1.

The Offense team chooses to Rush the ball again:

Roll one – **2**
The ball is moved forward 2 yards.

Roll two – **T**
First down is used and no further yards gained. The down marker is placed in hole 2.

Roll three – **T**
Second down is used and no further yards gained. The down marker is placed in hole 3.

Roll four – **3**
The ball is moved forward 3 yards.

Roll five – **T**
Third down is used and no further yards gained. The down marker is placed in hole 4.

Roll six – **3**
The ball is moved forward 3 yards.

Roll seven – **2**
The ball has reached the End Zone and scored a touchdown! 6 points are scored, and an extra point may be gained by a successful goal kick.

Play now passes to the other team.

CONSTRUCTION

Game board 12mm (½in) birch plywood 290mm (11⅜in) × 115mm (4½in).
Peg holes All peg holes are 3mm (⅛in) diameter.
Edging Wood effect self-adhesive plastic sheeting.
Pegs Three 30mm (1³⁄₁₆in) pegs.
Dice Five 18mm (¾in) dice.
Football The ball is shaped out of modelling clay and baked hard in an oven. A small hole is drilled partway into its middle, to allow a short piece of 3mm (⅛in) dowel rod to be glued into it. Prior to gluing, ensure that the dowel rod will easily fit into the centre peg holes on the game board. The 'lacing' on the ball is made using white transfer lines.

MARKING AND FINISHING

The board's touchlines, goal line, and yardage lines should be approximately 2mm (³⁄₃₂in) wide.

Only every fifth line need be marked, although the board shown has had every yard line marked with a thin line. This is optional, and has been done so as to allow easier yardage recognition – especially when the pace of the game becomes frantic!

The board is stained green and varnished.

The lettering and numbering are 12mm (½in) white transfers, except for the fourth down marker numbers, which are 5mm (⁷⁄₃₂in).

The Rushing Die is stained blue and marked with transfers:

1, 1, 2, 3, T, T

The Passing Die is stained orange and is marked with transfers:

C, C, INC, INC, INC, S

The Completion Die is stained red and is marked with transfers:

5, 10, 15, 20, 25, TD

The two remaining dice are left natural and are each marked:

1, 2, 3, 4, 5, 6

The three pegs are coloured orange.

Fig 19.1
End Zone game board.

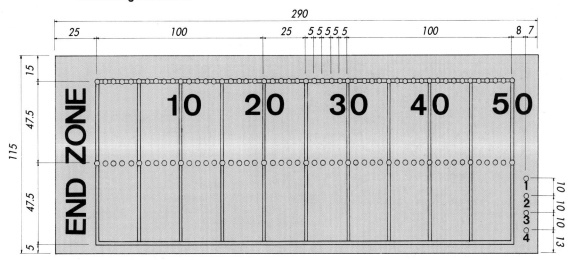

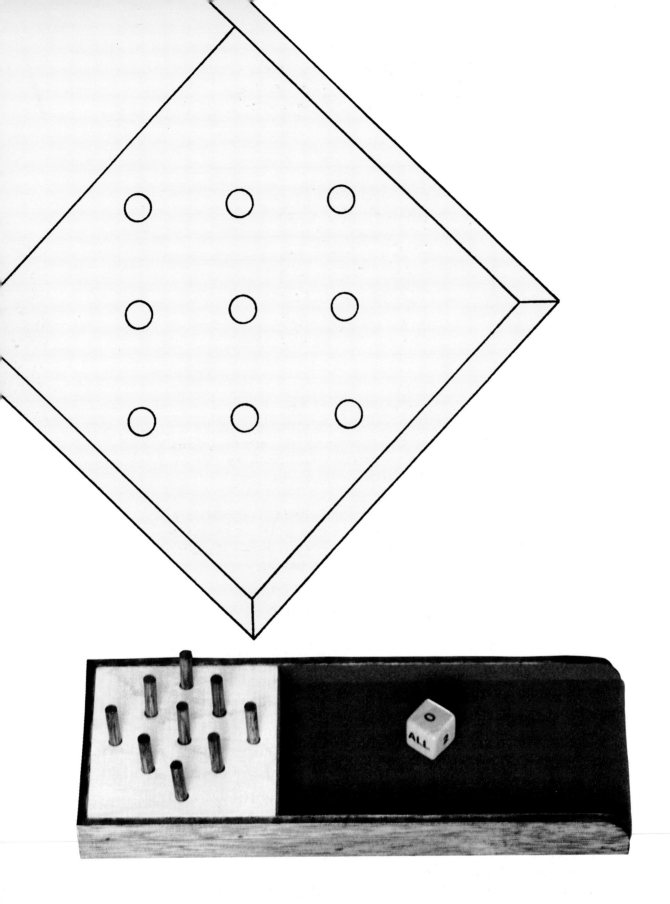

SKITTLES

INTRODUCTION

The ancient game of Skittles is still very popular in the authors' native West Country: almost every public house has a skittle alley which is in regular use.

This die and peg board version of the game has been designed to capture the essence of the actual game, and can be played as a team or an individual game; it would not be out of place in a bar or in the family home.

OBJECT OF THE GAME

To knock over as many skittles as possible in a given number of 'hands' (three rolls of the die).

FOR TWO OR MORE PLAYERS

EQUIPMENT

- Skittles game board
- Nine 'skittle' pegs
- One 'ball' die marked **0, 1, 2, 3, 4, ALL**
- Pencil and paper for scoring

PREPARATION

Place the nine skittle pegs into the nine holes on the skittle platforms.

Determine the order of play.

Draw up the scoresheet, putting the players' names in the correct order of play.

PLAY

Skittles can be played as either an individual or team game. The playing and scoring system is the same for both situations (see Fig 20.1).

Each player has six 'hands' in the game. Each hand consists of three rolls of the die, as with the ball in the actual game.

Play begins with the first player rolling the die on the 'alley' of the game board. If he rolls a number, he may remove that number of skittles from the game board. The player then rolls the die for a second and third time, on each roll removing the appropriate number of skittles.

If ALL is rolled, the player may remove all the skittles from the platform. When this is achieved on the first or second roll of the die, all nine skittles are replaced and the player rolls once or twice again to complete his hand.

Fig 20.1
Skittles scoresheet.

HOME TEAM						
PLAYER	HANDS					TOTAL
				GRAND TOTAL		

AWAY TEAM						
PLAYER	HANDS					TOTAL
				GRAND TOTAL		

If, for example, a 4 is rolled and there are only two skittles remaining on the game board, the two skittles are removed and two points are scored. If the player has any rolls left in that hand, all nine skittles are replaced and the next die roll is made. The player may not remove two of these replaced skittles to make the 4 rolled on the previous die roll.

After a player has completed his hand, his score is recorded on the scoresheet and the next player plays his first hand. After all the players have 'skittled' their first hand, play returns to the initial player, who skittles his second hand, and so on until all the players have each skittled six hands.

When playing Skittles as a team game, play alternates from team to team, e.g.:

Player one of Team A skittles his first hand
Player one of Team B skittles his first hand
Player two of Team A skittles his first hand, and so on.

The winner is the individual or team with the highest total score at the end of the game.

The game time may be shortened by reducing the number of hands played by each player.

CONSTRUCTION

Game board *Base:* 12mm (½in) birch plywood 247mm (9¾in) × 86mm (3⅜in).

Skittle platform: 12mm (½in) birch plywood 86mm (3⅜in) × 86mm (3⅜in) After the peg holes have been drilled into it, the skittle platform is glued on top of one end of the base board.

Peg holes Nine 6mm (¼in) peg holes are drilled into the skittle platform.

Edging 25mm (1in) × 5mm (³⁄₁₆in) ramin strip which is placed along three sides of the 'alley', leaving the short end furthest from the skittle platform open. The corners of the side edging are rounded at this end, so that the players' hands are not in danger of catching a sharp edge when rolling the die.

Pegs Nine 6mm (¼in) pegs for the skittles.

Dice One 18mm (¾in) die.

MARKING AND FINISHING

The skittles platform is left natural and varnished. The edging is coloured with a dark oak wood stain and varnished.

The alley is covered with self-adhesive green velour.

The skittles are coloured with the same dark oak wood stain used for the edging.

The die is left natural and, using 5mm (³⁄₁₆in) black transfers, marked as follows:

0, 1, 2, 3, 4, ALL

Fig 20.2
Skittles game board.

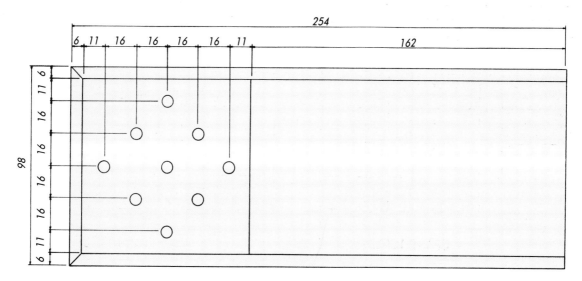

21

RACE DAY

INTRODUCTION

Fancy a day at the races? Well, here is your chance! In this simple but thrilling game each player takes the role of a racehorse owner.

The game is based on a flat race meeting consisting of six races. Each player has a horse or horses in each race of the day.

Prize money or points are awarded for second and third places, as well as first place, so it is possible to win the game without actually winning any races!

OBJECT OF THE GAME

To gain the most prize money or points at the end of the racing day of six races.

FOR TWO TO SIX PLAYERS

EQUIPMENT

- Race Day game board
- Six horses and jockeys
- One die marked with the colours of each horse
- 36 counters for prize money

ALLOCATION OF HORSES

For two players	Each player has three horses
For three players	Each player has two horses
*For four or five players	Each player has one horse
For six players	Each player has one horse

*Each player has one horse each, but the surplus horse or horses are still kept in the game and run. Any prize money or points that they may win is taken out of the game, and may not be claimed by any of the players.

PLAY

The horses are placed on the starting stall strip of their colour.

Each player takes it in turn to roll the die. The player who owns the red horse starts the first race;

the owner of the blue horse starts the second race and so on, through the colour sequence on the board.

Move the horse that corresponds with the colour rolled on the die one furlong (section) only. The horses must remain in their strip; they may not switch tracks.

The players continue to roll the die and move the horses, until three horses have claimed the first, second and third places. The prize money is then awarded.

After six races, total up each player's prize money or points, and the one with the most is the winner.

SCORING/PRIZES

The amount of prize money awarded at the end of each race is as follows:

First place .... three counters
Second place .... two counters
Third place .... one counter

ALTERNATIVES

There are five furlongs on the board shown in Fig 21.1. You may wish to make the board longer, increasing the number of furlongs raced. The race length could then be varied, e.g. a mile race (eight furlongs) could be followed by a five-furlong one, etc.

CONSTRUCTION

Game board 12mm (1/2in) birch plywood 350mm (13¾in) × 90mm (3¹⁷/₃₂in).
Edging 21mm (¹³/₁₆in) base moulding.
Horses Six horses are required: transfer the horse and jockey from Fig 21.2, copy six on to 6mm (¼in) birch plywood, and cut these out using a fretsaw (*see* Fig 2.3).
Dice One 18mm (¾in) die.

MARKING AND FINISHING

The game board consists of seven equal sections 50mm (2in) wide, which are divided into six equal strips 15mm (¹⁹/₃₂in) wide. There is one strip for each horse. Each section — excluding each end section — represents a furlong (220yds or 201.1m).

Each strip has a 10mm (³/₈in) diameter circle drawn in its centre at one end of the board; these circles represent the starting stalls. The circles are stained red, blue, yellow, green, orange and purple respectively.

The end strip at the opposite end of the board has a double penned line between it and the adjacent section: this represents the finishing line. The word FINISH is spelt out through the six strips at this end using 12mm (1/2in) transfers.

The board is left natural and varnished.

The edging is stained a mahogany colour using a wood stain, and then varnished.

The die has a 10mm (³/₈in) diameter circle penned on to each side. These circles are coloured to match the circles on the game board — one each of red, blue, yellow, green, orange and purple.

The horses are stained to match the colours of the circles on the die and game board. They are then varnished.

Fig 21.2
Side view of horse and jockey.

Fig 21.1
Race Day game board.

350							
47	3	50	50	50	50	50	50

Game © Jeff Loader 1993

22

VIKING VOYAGE

INTRODUCTION

Each player takes on the role of a Viking in command of a longboat. The crew have been adventuring for several months and are now returning to their homeland. However, they must first navigate around the fabled Fortune Islands and contend with the uncertainties of the elements. Will they have good fortune or foul?

OBJECT OF THE GAME

To be the first longboat to successfully reach the homeland.

FOR TWO TO FOUR PLAYERS

EQUIPMENT

- Viking Voyage game board
- Four longboats
- One movement die – marked **1, 2, 3, 4, 5, 6,** denoted by triangular 'pips'
- One weather die – marked **white cloud, black cloud, blank, blank, blank, blank**
- One fortune die – marked **1, 1, 1, 2, 2, 3,** denoted by triangular 'pips'

PLAY

Play starts in the bottom left playing square on the game board, marked with the large triangle – the start square.

The longboats follow the direction in which the triangles are pointing until they reach the home fjord (defined by a line at the base of its squares, which divides it from the rest of the game board) and, finally, the homeland, which is the top left-hand square on the board.

To reach the homeland, the exact number must be rolled.

The four Fortune Island squares to be found near the centre of the board must be counted and landed on in the same manner as any other square.

A TURN

Determine who starts the game by rolling the Movement Die; the highest score wins. Players take turns in the same order throughout the game.

A turn takes the following pattern:

The Movement Die and Weather Die are rolled together. The longboat is moved forward the number of squares indicated on the Movement Die.

The Weather Die is then considered, and the following action taken:

White cloud: a fair wind helps the longboat. The Fortune Die is rolled.
The longboat moves vertically upwards the number of rows indicated. A longboat may not enter the home fjord or reach the homeland if it is sent there by the Fortune Die. It must be placed outside these squares, on the row immediately below them.

Black cloud: a storm blows the longboat off course.
The Fortune Die is rolled.
The longboat moves vertically downwards the number of rows indicated. If a longboat is instructed to move down more rows than are available, it is then placed back on the start square.

Blank: no action is taken, and play passes to the next player.

THE FORTUNE ISLANDS

If a longboat lands on a Fortune Island, the Weather Die must be rolled until either a white or a black cloud comes up.

The Fortune Die is then rolled.

If a black cloud was rolled on the Weather Die, the player must miss the number of turns indicated on the Fortune Die.

If a white cloud was rolled on the Weather Die, the longboat is moved vertically upwards the number of rows indicated.

THE HOME FJORD

Only the Movement Die is rolled when a longboat is in the home fjord.

CONSTRUCTION

Game board 12mm ($\frac{1}{2}$in) birch plywood 250mm ($9\frac{5}{8}$in) × 250mm ($9\frac{5}{8}$in).
Edging 21mm ($1\frac{3}{16}$in) × 5mm ($\frac{7}{32}$in) ramin strip.
Longboats 6mm ($\frac{1}{4}$in) birch plywood: trace the outline from Fig 22.2, transfer it on to the plywood and cut out four longboats using a fretsaw.
Dice Three 18mm ($\frac{3}{4}$in) dice.

MARKING AND FINISHING

The playing area of the game board is divided with a rule and penned lines into 100 squares (10 × 10 grid). Each square is 23mm ($\frac{29}{32}$in) × 23mm ($\frac{29}{32}$in), making the total playing area 230mm ($9\frac{1}{16}$in) × 230mm ($9\frac{1}{16}$in). A border 10mm ($\frac{3}{8}$in) wide surrounds the grid (excluding edging).

One corner square should be chosen as the homeland; a 3mm ($\frac{1}{8}$in) wide line should run from the base of this square along the base of the adjacent five squares. These squares represent the home fjord.

Towards the centre of the game board there are four squares which contain irregular shapes, which represent the Fortune Islands. The outlines for these islands are drawn freehand with a pen.

The border pattern consists of a simple pattern of diamonds and triangles. (The inspiration for this came from a picture of an actual longboat, on which a similar pattern was carved.)

Before the sea is coloured, the home fjord line, border, and Fortune Island areas are given a couple of coats of varnish to seal them.

Paint the sea: we used a blue artists' acrylic, thinned and with a hint of green added. You will notice from the photographs that the depth of colour varies across the board, to suggest different depths of water. This has been achieved by applying progressively thicker mixes over an original thin coat in selected areas.

The Fortune Islands and the red border triangles are now painted.

The triangles (one per square) down the side squares of the grid on the game board indicate in which direction the longboats must sail. Triangles were chosen as they complement the border pattern, but arrows would be perfectly satisfactory.

The bottom left square (directly beneath the homeland square) should have a larger triangle, as it is the start square from which the longboats begin their voyage.

The triangles are dry rub-down transfers.

The edging is left natural and varnished.

The longboats are painted in bright gloss modellers' enamel paint.

The three dice are marked with the following symbols:

Movement Die	**1, 2, 3, 4, 5, 6**
Weather Die	**white cloud**
	black cloud
	four **blank** sides
Fortune Die	**1, 1, 1, 2, 2, 3**

All the numbers are represented by triangular 'pip' transfers.

The white and black clouds are painted on using modellers' enamel paint.

Fig 22.1
Viking Voyage game board.

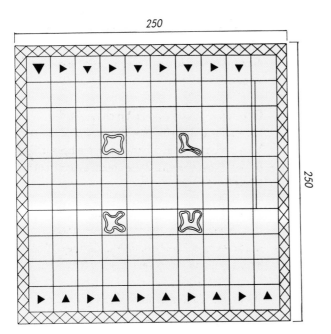

Fig 22.2
Side view of longboat.

Game © Jeff Loader 1993

23

HARRY'S GAME

INTRODUCTION

This game was named after one of our grandfathers, who enjoys playing games. Although based mainly on luck, the game provides many different options: players place stakes on the outcome of rolls of special dice.

OBJECT OF THE GAME

For the players to win all or as many counters as possible by staking their own counters on the outcome of the two dice.

FOR ANY NUMBER OF PLAYERS

EQUIPMENT

- Harry's Game game board
- Two dice marked **red, red, red, black, black, black. Heart, diamond, spade, club, O, DQ**
- An equal number of counters per player

PREPARATION

The minimum and maximum stakes should be decided, i.e. the minimum and maximum overall amount allowed to be staked by an individual player per turn, not the minimum or maximum staked on any one symbol.

To determine who will be the first Banker, the players each roll the die with the symbols on it until the O is rolled. The player making that roll is the Banker.

PLAY

The players (other than the Banker) place their counter/s on the symbols of their choice.

When all the stakes have been laid, the Banker rolls the two dice.

The Banker must pay out the following odds to any player who has staked his counters correctly on the outcome of the dice:

Red and black	PAY EVENS (the Banker matches the amount staked)
Diamond Heart Club Spade	PAY 4 – 1 (the Banker gives 4 counters to every one staked)

If O is rolled, the Banker wins all the stakes on the board and the bank passes to the player on the Banker's left.

When DQ is rolled, players must double their stakes on the board or quit. If they quit, the counters which they staked on the board go immediately to the Banker. The dice are then rolled again. If DQ comes up for a consecutive second time, it is ignored and the dice are re-rolled.

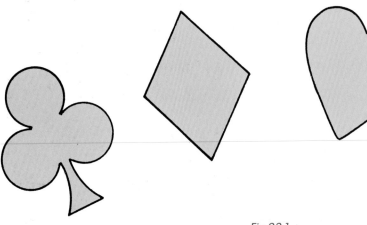

Fig 23.1
Symbols for game board.

CONSTRUCTION

Game board 12mm (½in) birch plywood 202mm (8in) × 202mm (8in).
Edging 21mm (1³⁄₁₆in) base moulding.
Dice Two 18mm (¾in) dice.

MARKING AND FINISHING

Mark out and pen the lines which divide the game board into sections.

The red and black areas are painted using modeller's matt enamel paint. These areas could be stained, but beware of the colours becoming too 'wishy-washy'. The bold red and black also make the surrounding natural wood grain stand out.

To mark the symbols, either trace the shapes from Fig 23.1 and then transfer them straight on to the game board's surface, using French curves, circle template and rule, or trace the shapes on to some hardboard and cut them out to use as templates.

The symbols are painted in the same way as the red and black areas.

The edging is painted black.

The game board and edging are both varnished.

The dice are painted white for contrast.

One die has three sides painted red and three sides black; the other is marked with a red diamond, red heart, black spade, black club (all painted on), 'O' and 'DQ' (transfers).

Fig 23.2
Harry's Game game board.

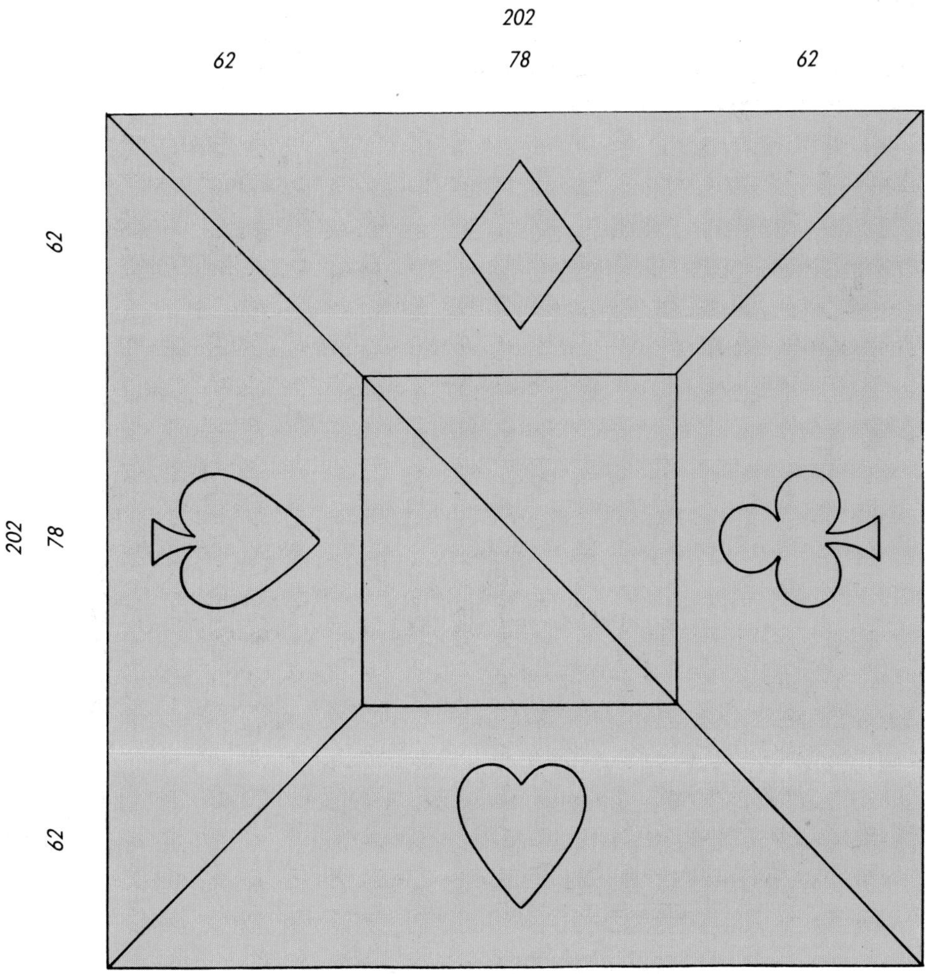

202

62   78   62

62

202   78

62

105

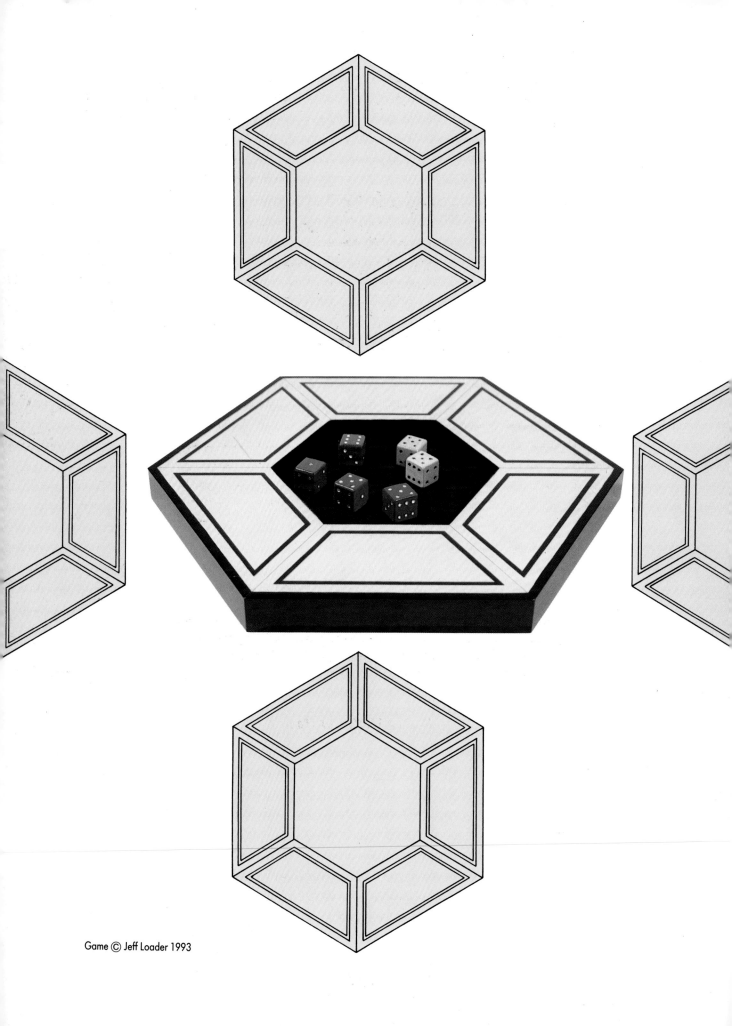

24

MONTE CARLO

INTRODUCTION

In this straightforward, fast-paced game, players try to beat the Bank. Each player rolls a die and must place a stake on the probability of it beating the Banker's die roll. If dissatisfied with this first die roll, the players may 'buy' a second roll. However, this could prove risky, as they could finish their turn with a worse score!

OBJECT OF THE GAME

Each player rolls a die and places a bet on the probability of his score beating that of the Banker. The player winning the most counters at the end of an agreed time period or number of rounds is the winner.

FOR TWO TO SIX PLAYERS

EQUIPMENT

- Monte Carlo game board
- Two dice, each marked **1, 2, 3, 4, 5, 6,** per player
- An equal number of counters per player

PREPARATION

Determine first which player is to be the Banker. All players roll both their dice, and the highest score wins.

Determine the length of the game, either in time or the number of rounds to be played.

If desired, the players should agree the minimum and maximum stakes allowable throughout the game.

PLAY

Each player is allotted a segment of the Monte Carlo game board. After completing a die roll, each player places his die, rolled side uppermost, on to his own segment: this ensures that all rolls are clearly visible to all players in the game. Any stakes which a player may place are also displayed on this segment. The actual die rolls are made into the central tray of the board.

The player to the left of the Banker begins play by rolling one of his dice. He then places a stake (counters) on the result.

If he is dissatisfied with the result of the first die roll (usually if it is a low score), he may 'buy' another die roll for the same price as the original stake. In this instance, the player rolls his second die.

If the same score is rolled again (a double), the player instantly beats the Banker, who has to pay him evens, i.e. the Banker matches the player's stakes. This player now takes no further part in this round of the game.

The player must accept whatever score is rolled on the second die, and must keep that score. The first die is removed from the board. Sometimes the second score is lower than the first, so players must choose carefully!

Play moves in a clockwise direction around the game board until every player has had their turn. The Banker then rolls his die. He may only roll one die, and is not given the option of a second die roll.

If the Banker rolls:

1 The same number or higher than any, or all, of the players, he wins the counters they have staked.
2 A lower number than any, or all, of the players, he must pay them winnings equal to their stake.
3 A 6, all the players must pay him double their stake. The only exception to this rule is that any players who also scored a 6 only lose their stake, and do not have to double it.

The Bank changes after each round, and the player to the Banker's left becomes the new Banker.

CONSTRUCTION

Game board 12mm (½in) birch plywood: two hexagonal pieces measuring 320mm (12⁹/₁₆in) from opposite point to point. The top piece has a smaller hexagonal section cut from its centre using a fretsaw, and when the two pieces are glued together the central hexagonal cutaway becomes a tray (see Fig 24.1). 'Clean up' the edges of the game board to leave them smooth.

There are several ways to mark out the hexagon; one of the easiest is to use a rule, compass and/or a protractor. If using a protractor, remember that each internal angle of the hexagon is 120°.

Edging 25mm (1in) × 6mm (¼in) ramin strip. The edging will require 60° mitres, not the usual 45° – cut one or two 60° slots in a bench hook to act as a saw guide.

Dice Each player uses two 18mm (¾in) dice, so a maximum of 12 will be required.

MARKING AND FINISHING

The game board is divided into six equal sections by drawing lines between opposing points.

Each section has an internal decorative border 3mm (⅛in) wide. These borders are set 7mm (⁹/₃₂in) in from the section perimeters.

Both the decorative borders and the edging are painted black.

After final varnishing, the central tray of the game board is lined with black velour.

The dice may be of any colour, and should each be marked **1, 2, 3, 4, 5, 6.**

Fig 24.1
Monte Carlo and Dog and Duck game board.

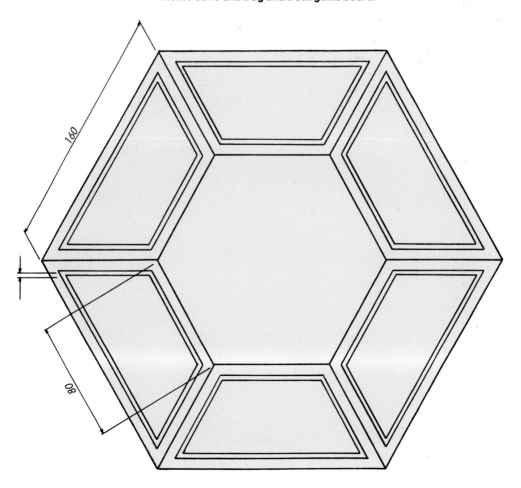

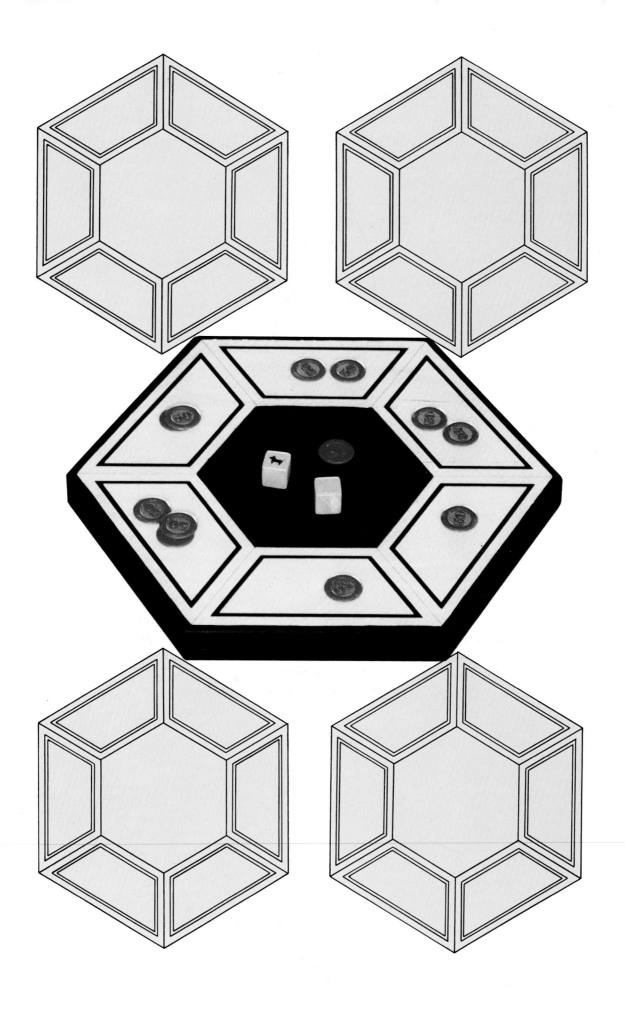

25

DOG AND DUCK

INTRODUCTION

In this fun game, the Monte Carlo game board is used as a pond and bank. Each player starts with two counters placed on a segment of the game board, the bank. Two dice marked with a dog and a duck symbol are used: by rolling the dice, the players make the ducks dive into the pond and the dogs chase around the bank!

OBJECT OF THE GAME

By rolling the dice, the players either pass the counters around the game board (the dogs) or put them into the central tray (the ducks in the pond). The winner of the game, and the contents of the pond, is the last player to retain a counter and make three dice rolls without rolling a dog!

FOR TWO TO SIX PLAYERS

EQUIPMENT

- Monte Carlo game board
- Two dice, each marked with a dog, a duck and four blank sides
- Two counters per player

PLAY

Each player is allotted a segment of the game board, on which he places his two counters. Play moves in a clockwise direction.

Players take it in turns to roll the two dice once:

If a duck is rolled, the player must put a counter into the pond.

If two ducks are rolled, the player must put two counters into the pond.

If a dog is rolled, the player must pass a counter (the dog) to the player on his left.

If two dogs are rolled, the player must pass two counters to the player on his left. If he only has one counter left, this will suffice.

If a dog and a duck are rolled and the player has only one counter left the dog takes priority and the counter is passed to the player on his left.

If a player has no counters left, he may not roll the dice but passes them on.

When there is only one player left with a counter, he must roll the two dice three times without rolling a dog. If he does this, he wins the counters in the pond. However, if he is unsuccessful, the counter and the two dice pass to the player on his left. This player now attempts to do the same, and so on until the counters in the pond are won.

CONSTRUCTION

Game board Details for the construction of the Monte Carlo game board are given in Chapter 24.
Dice Two 18mm (¾in) dice.

MARKING AND FINISHING

The game board is marked as for the game of Monte Carlo.

The dice are left natural and varnished before painting a black dog on one side and a yellow duck on another side of each one. The other four sides are left natural.

A protective coat of varnish is then applied.

An alternative to painting the symbols of a dog and a duck is to use transfers to spell out the words DOG and DUCK.

26

CROWN AND ANCHOR

INTRODUCTION

This game is best known as being popular with British seamen, who often marked the playing surface on to a piece of cloth. In the forces Crown and Anchor was often a prohibited game, making the cloth board ideal — it could be quickly gathered up and hidden inside a jacket if the game was in danger of discovery.

Our personal connection with the game is through one of our grandfathers, who used to play the game in the Army. It was often played on pay day. Pay for a private was then (c.1940) 14 shillings (70p) per week, and it was known for some soldiers to stake a full week's pay on one turn!

A simplified board for the game may be made by substituting numbers (1—6) for the symbols (*see* Fig 26.1). Three standard dice (marked 1—6) can then be used.

OBJECT OF THE GAME

To win counters by placing bets on the different symbols of the game board.

FOR ANY NUMBER OF PLAYERS

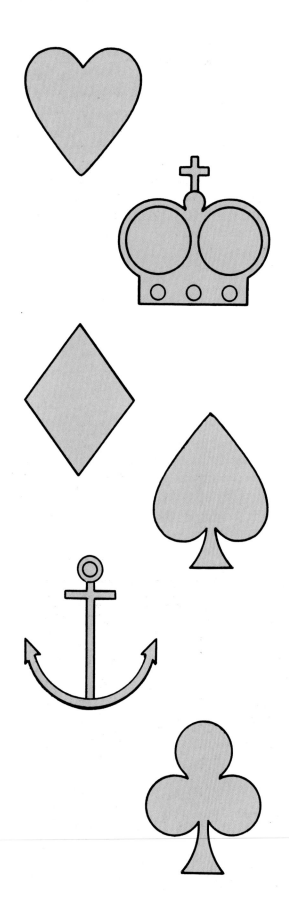

EQUIPMENT

- Crown and Anchor game board
- Three dice, each marked heart, crown, diamond, spade, anchor, club
- An equal number of counters per player

PLAY

Before starting play, one player is nominated to be the initial Banker. After each round the Bank will pass to the next player on the left (a round is one throw of the dice); this is because the Banker has a slight advantage.

Play begins by all the players except the Banker placing stakes on the symbols of their choice. The Banker then rolls the three dice together.

The Banker then pays out on each of the symbols rolled at the following rates:

Singles	Evens
Doubles	2 – 1
Three of a kind	3 – 1

Any stakes placed on symbols that are not rolled are claimed by the Banker.

Players must retire from the game when they have no counters left.

The game may be stopped at any time agreed by the players.

CONSTRUCTION

Game board 12mm (½in) birch plywood 257mm (10⅛in) × 178mm (7in).
Edging 21mm (¹³⁄₁₆in) base moulding.
Dice Three 18mm (¾in) dice.

Fig 26.1
Crown and Anchor symbols.

MARKING AND FINISHING

The lines dividing the game board into six playing areas should be drawn first.

Each symbol may be traced from Fig 26.1 and placed in the centre of the relevant section. A combination of rule, French curves, and circle template is helpful when inking over these symbols.

After sealing the game board with varnish, all the red and black areas (including the section dividing lines) are painted.

A finishing coat of varnish should then be applied.

The dice are left natural and varnished.

The symbols are then applied: the heart, diamond, spade and club are fairly straightforward to paint.

The Crown and Anchor symbols may also be painted, but this requires a very steady hand! An alternative to this – the one we used – is to apply a combination of transfers, e.g. the Anchor top ring is a letter 'o', its centre bars are letter 'L's, and its base is from a bracket and two letter 'v's. Any area where the transfers do not quite meet can be touched in with paint.

Fig 26.2
Crown and Anchor game board.

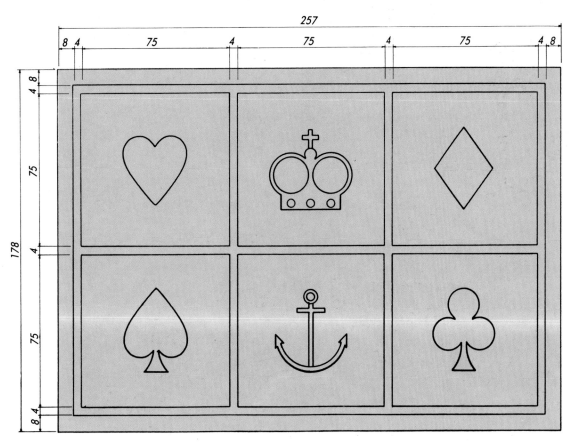

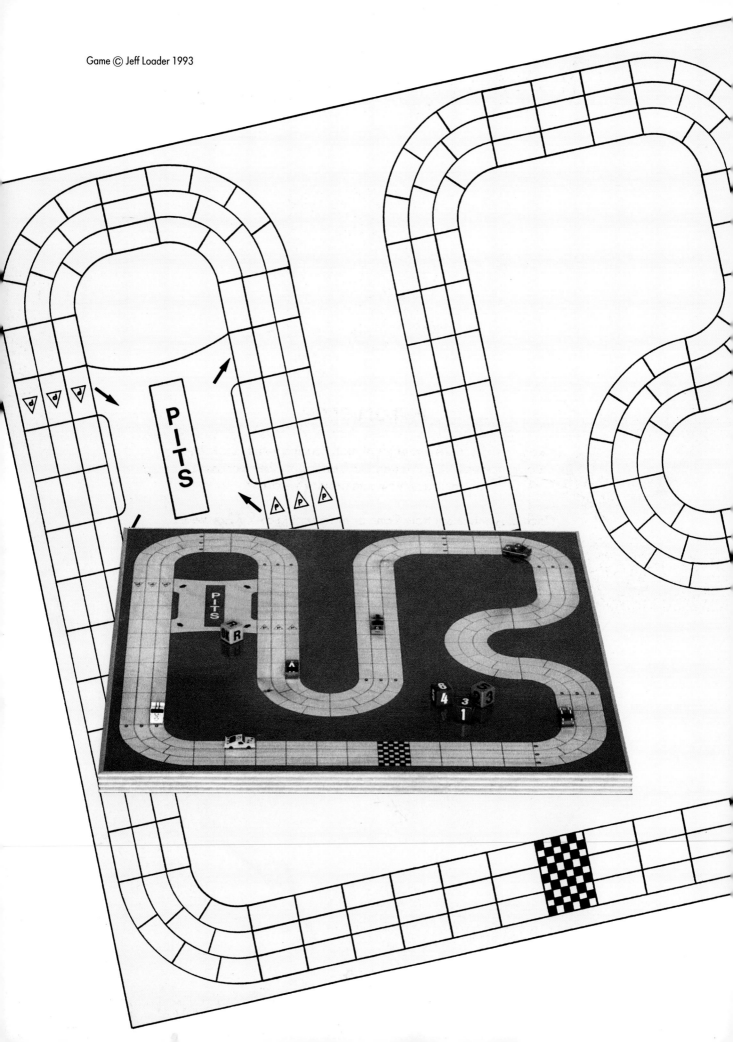

PITS

27

MOTOR RACING

INTRODUCTION

Recreate the thrills and spills of motor racing with this exciting board game. Skill, tactics and luck each play their part as the players race their cars around the circuit.

Each player has control of one or more racing cars. By strategic use of the Speed Dice, the cars must negotiate the twists and turns of the track without losing position by spinning off or taking an ill-timed pit stop.

OBJECT OF THE GAME

Each player is in control of a racing car or cars. The cars race around the circuit for a predetermined number of laps. The car which crosses the finishing line first is the winner of the race.

FOR TWO TO SIX PLAYERS

EQUIPMENT

- Motor Racing game board
- Six racing cars (the racing circuit is large enough to take 12 cars if desired)
- Three Speed Dice:
  Fast Die (red) — **6, 6, 5, 4, 4, 2**
  Medium Die (orange) — **5, 4, 3, 3, 2, 1**
  Slow Die (green) — **3, 2, 2, 1, 1, 1**
- One Pit Stop Die (natural) — **T, T, T, R, R, OK**

PREPARATION

Decide how many laps of the circuit have to be completed before the race ends — two is a good number when first playing the game.

PLAY

Place the racing cars on the starting grid (chequered squares). If more than three cars are competing, the other cars are placed behind on the next row. As the most advantageous starting position (pole position) is the inside chequered square, determine which car will get which starting position. Drawing lots, i.e. using playing

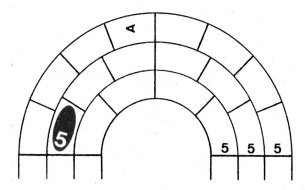

Fig 27.1
Car 5 spins off on corner square; it must re-enter on square A.

cards numbered 1–6, is a good way of doing this.

MOVEMENT OF CARS

The cars are moved according to the roll made on one of the Speed Dice, which represent the speed at which a car is travelling; 6 represents the fastest speed possible, and 1 the slowest. The choice of

which die is to be rolled at any particular point of the racing track is entirely the decision of the player whose turn it is.

When a die is rolled, the relevant car is moved the number of squares shown on the die. The cars race around the track in an anticlockwise direction.

CORNERS AND CORNERING

The corners are graded by degrees of severity, either 5 or 6. The first row of three playing squares of each corner, or series of corners, is marked with a 5 or a 6. This represents the speed at which a car will spin off the track, e.g. a car entering a bend graded 5 on a die roll (or speed) of 5 or 6 will spin off the track.

A car will also spin off if the graded speed or faster is rolled whilst the car is on any part of the bend, including the last playing square.

The penalty for spinning off is as follows:

Grade 5 bend .... miss 2 turns
Grade 6 bend .... miss 1 turn

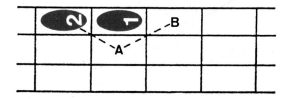

Fig 27.2
Car 2 may overtake car 1 by moving to square B via square A.

After missing the appropriate number of turns, the car may re-enter the track on the rear outside playing square of the bend. This playing square is counted as part of the die roll.

On a series of bends, the re-entry point will be at the rear outside playing square of the particular bend section from which the car spun off (*see* Fig 27.1).

If the usual re-entry playing square is occupied, re-entry may take place on the next vacant playing square on the outside lane of the track behind it.

MANOEUVRING IN A GROUP AND OVERTAKING

A simple overtaking manoeuvre is shown in Fig 27.2.

Fig 27.3 shows an instance where a car may not overtake because another car is boxing it in. In this example, the white car would have to remain behind the black car until either the black or striped car is moved.

A car may never be moved sideways, even if it means that it will otherwise become boxed in (*see* Fig 27.4).

PIT STOPS

When a car finishes moving and lands on a playing square marked with a pit stop symbol (P), the Pit Stop Die must be immediately rolled.

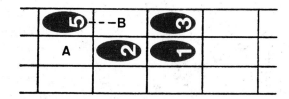

Fig 27.3
Car 4 may not go to square B via square A, as car 5 is boxing it in.

If T is rolled, the car must go directly into the pits for a tyre change. MISS 1 TURN.

If R is rolled, the car must go directly into the pits for repairs. MISS 2 TURNS.

If OK is rolled, the fault has rectified itself and the car may continue the race on its next turn.

Cars forced to make a pit stop re-enter the track on the square indicated. If this square is occupied, the car must miss another turn until it is free.

TACTICS

When driving around a corner, it is best to keep the car on the inside of the three lanes.

To improve your chances of winning, it may be necessary to take some risks when choosing which Speed Die to roll. This is the key element of the game: overcaution, even though your car will rarely spin off, will usually result in losing the race, while recklessness with the use of the Fast Die will result in numerous turns missed due to spinoffs. A happy medium needs to be found between the two to ensure victory. Choose wisely!

PLAY ALTERNATIVE

Players may wish to race two cars at a time, thus creating a racing team. A series of races over a varying number of laps, with a points system for each race, could be created, with the winner over, for example, six races being the team with the

Fig 27.4
Car 5 may not move sideways on to square A; it may only move to square B.

most points. A suggested points system (for six cars in three teams) is shown below:

1st place	8 points
2nd place	6 points
3rd place	4 points
4th place	3 points
5th place	2 points
6th place	1 point

CONSTRUCTION

Game board 12mm (½in) birch plywood 500mm (19¹¹⁄₁₆in) × 500mm (19¹¹⁄₁₆in).
Edging 21mm (⁷⁄₃₂in) reed moulding.
Racing cars These are fretsawed from beech. Transfer the side profile from Fig 27.5 on to the wood; if this shape proves difficult to cut out, a simple wedge design could be used as an alternative.
Dice Four 18mm (¾in) dice.

MARKING AND FINISHING

The racing circuit is straightforward to reproduce if a grid is first drawn lightly in pencil on to the game board. This grid is made up of 15mm (¹⁹⁄₃₂in) × 15mm (¹⁹⁄₃₂in) squares. On the straight sections of the track, each playing square measures 30mm (1³⁄₁₆in) × 15mm (¹⁹⁄₃₂in) – two squares of the grid.

Each bend, or series of bends, is made up from 90° corner sections.

Templates to assist with the marking of these corner sections can be made and then drawn around: these templates, made from hardboard, consist of four circles of the following diameters: 60mm (2³⁄₈in), 90mm (3¹⁷⁄₃₂in), 120mm (4¾in) and 150mm (5¹³⁄₁₆in).

Each 90° corner section is subdivided. The inside lane consists of two playing squares, the middle lane three playing squares and the outside lane four playing squares. Use a protractor to plot where the divisions must be marked at the following angles:

Inside lane   – 45°
Middle lane – 30° and 60°
Outside lane – 22.5°, 45° and 67.5°

The start and finish playing squares are chequered with 5mm (⁷⁄₃₂in) squares.

Seal the racing circuit with varnish prior to staining the rest of the game board (or grass) green.

Transfers are used to label the pits and number the spin-off speeds of the corners on the track. The track pit stop symbols are triangle transfers with the letter P placed inside.

The edging is left natural.

The game board and edging are varnished.

The cars are painted with hobbyist enamels and decorated with transfers. They are given a top coat of varnish for protection.

The dice are coloured: one each of red, orange, green and natural. They are marked as follows:

Red   – **6, 6, 5, 4, 4, 2**
Orange – **5, 4, 3, 3, 2, 1**
Green   – **3, 2, 2, 1, 1, 1**
Natural – **T, T, T, R, R, OK**

Fig 27.5
Side view of racing car.

Fig 27.6
Motor Racing game board.

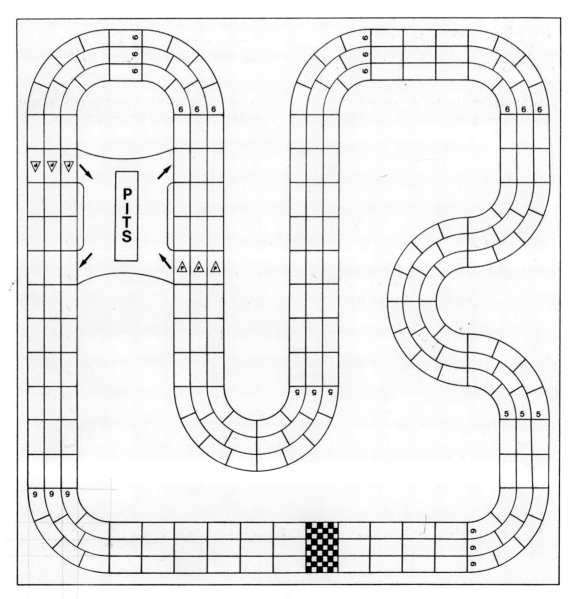

123

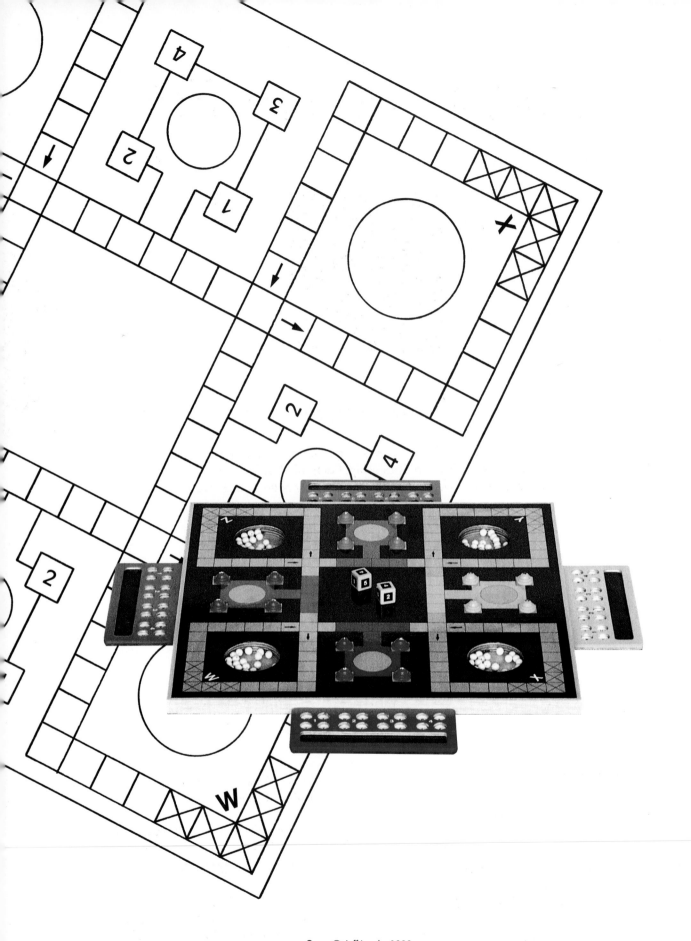

28

GALACTIC PIRATES

INTRODUCTION

In this game each player becomes the ruthless commander of a large Pirate Trading Spaceship. Each ship has four small spacecraft which are sent out to peaceably collect cargo from trading planets.

However, each avaricious commander yearns to be the richest and most powerful in the Galaxy. To achieve their ambitions, they resort to acts of piracy and raid each others' spacecrafts.

OBJECT OF THE GAME

To be the commander of the Pirate Trading Spaceship which has collected the most cargo units at the end of the game.

FOR TWO TO FOUR PLAYERS

EQUIPMENT

● Galactic Pirates game board. The four large Pirate Trading Spaceships are coloured orange, red, yellow and blue respectively. Each has four numbered squares, the launch pads, from which its four small cargo collecting spacecraft are launched.

Four of the playing squares immediately in front of each Pirate Trading Spaceship are coloured the same as the Ship; these are its Landing Platform.

Towards each corner of the game board are four circular trays. These are the planets where the cargo (represented by beads) is kept.

Around each planet is the Galactic Pathway of playing squares which link all parts of Space (the game board) to each other. The playing

squares, marked **X** and situated in the outer corners of the Galactic Pathway, are the planet's pick-up squares.
- Four cargo holds. Each Pirate Trading Spaceship has a separate cargo hold in which the cargo that has been collected is recorded and stored.

The 16 small holes represent the cargo holds of the small spacecraft, and the long, rectangular tray represents the main cargo hold of the Pirate Trading Spaceship.
- Four spacecraft per Pirate Trading Spaceship; each set is numbered **1, 2, 3, 4**
- 80 cargo units beads
- Two dice each marked **1, 2, 3, 4, 5, 6**

PREPARATION

Each player chooses one Pirate Trading Spaceship and places its four spacecraft on the appropriate launch pads.

20 units of cargo are placed into each planet.

Determine which player will start the game by each player rolling the two dice once. The player with the highest total score starts the game. Play moves in a clockwise direction.

PLAY

MOVEMENT

Movement around the central square of the Galactic Pathway can be in any direction. Movement along the part of the Galactic Pathway which surrounds each planet is restricted to one direction only: the arrows on the playing squares indicate the direction which must be taken.

Movement is determined by a roll of the two dice. The combined total rolled indicates the number of playing squares which one spacecraft must move. The total may not be split between two spacecraft, and the dice roll must be acted upon if a spacecraft is free to move.

If more than one spacecraft from any particular Pirate Trading Spaceship is on the Galactic

Pathway, the player may choose which spacecraft moves.

If a double is rolled on the dice it is counted and used as any other dice roll, except that the player who rolled it then receives a second roll.

A double must be rolled to launch a spacecraft on to the Galactic Pathway; the spacecraft is then moved the number of playing squares indicated by the dice out of the mother Pirate Trading Spaceship, along the Galactic Pathway. The first square to be counted is always one of the two centre squares of the Pirate Trading Spaceship's Landing Platform. The player then makes another roll of the dice, as a double always results in another go.

A player may choose not to launch a spacecraft when he rolls a double if he already has one or more spacecraft launched.

Upon return to the Pirate Trading Spaceship, a spacecraft does not have to roll the exact number on the dice in order to land. Provided that the dice roll moves the spacecraft on to a square of the appropriate Landing Platform, it is said to have 'docked', and the spacecraft is placed on its launch pad.

THE SPACECRAFT

On any flight from its mother Pirate Trading Spaceship, it is the duty of each spacecraft to visit each of the W, X, Y and Z planets and collect cargo.

Each spacecraft can only carry one unit of cargo from each planet in its hold at any one time, so once it has visited each planet it must return to the Pirate Trading Spaceship, to unload and store the cargo prior to setting out again.

COLLECTING CARGO UNITS FROM THE PLANETS

To collect cargo from the planets, a spacecraft must finish a move by landing on one of the planet pick-up squares (marked X).

If the spacecraft overshoots the pick-up squares, it is unable to collect cargo and must move around the planet again and try to land successfully on the second attempt.

If a spacecraft lands on an occupied pick-up square it may not collect cargo, but must take off and move around the Galactic Pathway on its next move.

USING THE CARGO HOLDS

Each cargo hold contains 16 small circular holes – four for each spacecraft. The number of the spacecraft which each group of holes represents is found in the middle of its four holes. The letter of the planet from which the cargo must be obtained is in each hole, so a piece of cargo obtained at planet Y by Spacecraft 2 would go into the hole marked Y closest to the number 2.

When all four of a spacecraft's holds contain a unit of cargo, it must return to its mother Pirate Trading Spaceship and unload. The unloaded cargo goes directly into the Pirate Trading Spaceship's cargo hold, represented by the large rectangular tray located beneath the four sets of spacecraft cargo holds.

RAIDING A SPACECRAFT

Any spacecraft which carries cargo is prey to any spacecraft from another Pirate Trading Spaceship.

A spacecraft with some or all of its cargo holds empty may attempt to 'raid' a spacecraft which has cargo, and may claim that cargo as its own.

In order to raid, the attacking spacecraft must finish a move by landing on exactly the same playing square as the victim spacecraft.

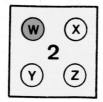
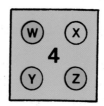

Fig 28.1
Cargo holds of yellow and green spacecraft.

Fig 28.2
Cargo holds.

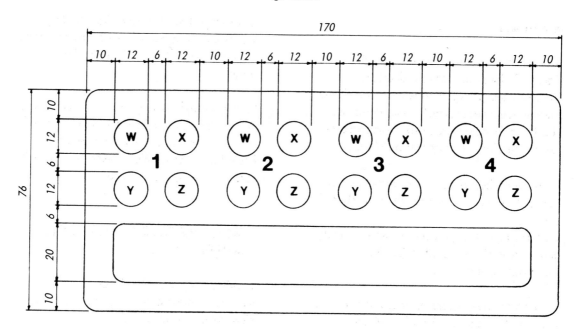

Any cargo units which the victim spacecraft is carrying are immediately captured by the attacking spacecraft, which places them into its own cargo hold. For example: yellow spacecraft 2 raids green spacecraft 4 (see Fig 28.1).

The yellow spacecraft may take the green spacecraft's Y and Z cargo and put them in its own cargo hold; the W cargo cannot be claimed, as no spacecraft may carry more than one piece of cargo from the same planet at any one time. The W unit of cargo is thus replaced into the planet W.

The now empty green spacecraft must return directly (with no dice rolls required) to the mother Pirate Trading Spaceship, and may then be relaunched in the usual way.

No spacecraft can be raided whilst it is on a planet's pick-up square.

A spacecraft cannot be raided whilst it is on its own mother Pirate Trading Spaceship's Landing Platform.

A spacecraft which is raided but does not have any cargo is simply returned directly to its mother Pirate Trading Spaceship.

THE END OF THE GAME

The game ends when:

1 It is not possible for any spacecraft to carry back any full loads of cargo to the mother Pirate Trading Spaceship.
2 A predetermined period of time (for example, one hour) has elapsed.

THE WINNER

The winner of the game is the player who has the most units of cargo in the hold of his Pirate Trading Spaceship. Any units of cargo still on the spacecraft do not count towards this total.

CONSTRUCTION

Game board 12mm ($\frac{1}{2}$in) birch plywood 420mm (16$\frac{9}{16}$in) × 420mm (16$\frac{9}{16}$in). To find the correct positions for the planet holes, mark out the game board layout in pencil (see Marking and Finishing below).

The planets (four circular trays) are cut out using a brace and expansive bit set for 60mm (2$\frac{3}{8}$in) diameter. Before cutting with the expansive bit, it is helpful to drill a small pilot hole no bigger than 3mm ($\frac{1}{8}$in) at the centre point of each planet: this will help keep the bit central while boring the hole.

When the lead screw starts to break through the back of the board, it is advisable to stop boring, remove the bit and start boring again from the back of the board: this will help prevent the grain splitting out when boring through. Once cut, sand the holes smooth with abrasive paper. The four planet holes are backed with squares of 3mm ($\frac{1}{8}$in) birch plywood.
Edging 21mm (1$\frac{3}{16}$in) × 5mm ($\frac{7}{32}$in) ramin strip.
Spacecraft Sixteen 20mm ($\frac{25}{32}$in) diameter shaped turnings, the type used for wooden toy hubcaps.
Cargo Eighty 10mm ($\frac{3}{8}$in) diameter beads.
Dice Two 18mm ($\frac{3}{4}$in) dice.
Cargo holds Four are required.
Base: 170mm (6$\frac{11}{16}$in) × 76mm (3in) hardboard
Top: 3mm ($\frac{1}{8}$in) birch plywood 170mm (6$\frac{11}{16}$in) × 76mm (3in)
Before gluing the base and top together, the 16 small spacecraft cargo holds are drilled out of the top piece using a 12mm ($\frac{1}{2}$in) spade bit. The long, rectangular main cargo hold is also cut out, using a fretsaw (see Fig 28.2).

MARKING AND FINISHING

Plotting the game layout on to the game board can be simplified by gridding the board lightly with a pencil and rule into 20mm ($\frac{25}{32}$in) × 20mm ($\frac{25}{32}$in) squares. By referring to Fig 28.3 it will then be straightforward to plot the layout on to the grid.

All areas to be left natural are first varnished, to seal them.

Each of the four Pirate Trading Spaceships is stained its chosen colour, as are the four playing squares on the Galactic Pathway closest to the entrance of each ship (these are the Landing Platforms).

The background of the game board (Space) is coloured a dark blue/black.

The **W, X, Y,** and **Z** letters which identify each planet are 12mm (½in) white transfers.

The numbers of each small spacecraft launch pad are 8mm (⁵⁄₁₆in) transfers.

The directional arrows on the Galactic Pathway are black transfers.

The edging is left natural.

The game board and edging are varnished.

The four cargo holds are coloured the same as their mother Pirate Trading Spaceships. The 16 small cargo holds are lettered with 3mm (⅛in) transfers and numbered with 5mm (⁷⁄₃₂in) transfers.

The spacecraft are coloured to match their mothership, four per Pirate Trading Spaceship. They are numbered using 5mm (⁷⁄₃₂in) transfers, and varnished.

Each of the two dice is marked **1, 2, 3, 4, 5** and **6**. The dice are left natural, and a black transfer square is used on each side under 5mm (⁷⁄₃₂in) white transfer numbers. They are then varnished.

Fig 28.3
Galactic Pirates game board.

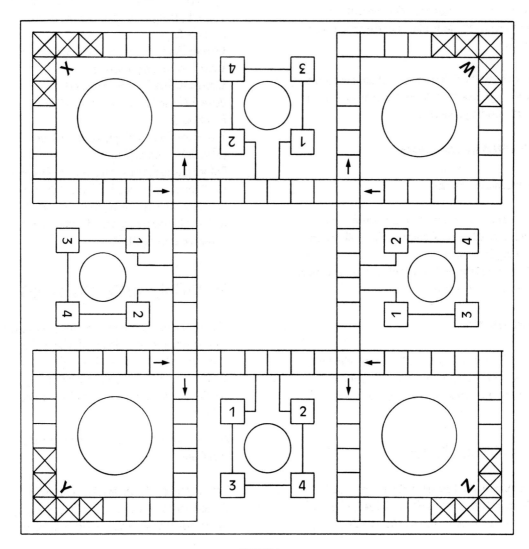

129

Game © Jeff Loader 1993

29

KNIGHTS OF THE ROUND TABLE

INTRODUCTION

Based upon myths and legends from the authors' home town, this game has been devised to appeal to players of all ages.

The land is threatened by an evil Black Baron. The task of defeating him has been given to the Knights of the Round Table. To ensure success in their mission, the Knights must travel throughout the land, visiting its castles where they gain wisdom and skills, thereby improving their experience. Each Knight must use his own discretion to decide how much experience he requires before engaging the Black Baron in battle. The more experience gained, the greater the chance of defeating him.

Having heard of the Knights' task, the Black Baron sends forth his own powerful envoy, the Black Knight, to fight and hinder them on their quest.

OBJECT OF THE GAME

Each player is one of The Knights of the Round Table. It is each Knight's duty to travel forth, gain experience, avoid or fight the Black Knight, and be the Knight that successfully defeats the Black Baron.

FOR TWO TO SIX PLAYERS

EQUIPMENT

- Knights of the Round Table game board. The outer playing area has three types of playing squares: blank squares – ordinary playing squares without special note; six castle squares, positioned at regular intervals at the end of the paths radiating from the centre of the board; three trap squares, each marked with a cross.
- Six Knights of the Round Table, one playing piece per player
- The Black Knight
- Experience card, for recording the progress of the Knights of the Round Table during the game
- Two dice, each marked **1, 2, 3, 4, 5, 6**

PREPARATION

The Black Knight is placed in the centre circle of the game board – the Black Baron's lair.

Each Knight of the Round Table in use is placed on a castle square of the player's choice, only one Knight per castle square.

A player is nominated or chosen by the roll of a die to be the scorekeeper.

Each Knight of the Round Table always starts the quest with two experience points, which are recorded on the experience card (*see* p. 134).

The Black Baron's strength remains constant throughout the game, and is as follows:

For two players .... 8 points
For three players .... 8 points
For four players .... 8 points
For five players .... 6 points
For six players .... 6 points

The Black Knight does not gain or lose any points throughout the game.

PLAY

The Knights of the Round Table
The objective of a Knight of the Round Table is to

move around the board, gaining experience points with which to fight and overcome the evil Black Baron.

Each player has sole control of one Knight of the Round Table, which may only move in a clockwise direction around the board, until challenging the Black Baron, when he moves to the centre of the board.

One die (marked 1–6) is used to move the Knights; if a six is thrown, another turn must be taken.

The Black Knight
The objective of the Black Knight is to protect the Black Baron by preventing the Knights of the Round Table from gaining experience points. He does this by landing on the same square as a Knight of the Round Table and engaging him in battle, in order to steal some of his points.

The Black Knight is controlled by each player in turn, including turns during which any player's Knight is restricted from moving. The Black Knight can move both clockwise and anticlockwise.

Two dice (each marked 1–6) are used to move the Black Knight. The total score of the two dice may be used in a number of ways, e.g.:

3 + 5 = 8 spaces in one direction only

3 + 5 = 3 spaces clockwise and 5 spaces
      anticlockwise
      or
      5 spaces clockwise and 3 spaces
      anticlockwise

The Black Knight does not receive another throw if a double or a six is thrown.

Neither the Knights of the Round Table nor the Black Knight may move across the centre of the board – all play must take place on the circumference of the board. The two exceptions to this are when a Knight of the Round Table wishes to challenge the Black Baron, and at the start of the game, when the Black Knight moves from his starting point at the centre of the board to join the Knights of the Round Table on the playing circle.

A TURN

A turn consists of a player rolling one die for, and moving, their own Knight of the Round Table, immediately followed by rolling two dice for, and moving, the Black Knight.

The castles

When a player lands on:

An unoccupied castle, he automatically gains two experience points.

A castle occupied by another player, he automatically gains two experience points.

A castle occupied by the Black Knight, he may not gain any experience points, even after the Black Knight has moved to another space. However, he does not have to fight or give any experience points to the Black Knight.

When a player is already on a castle and the Black Knight lands on the same castle, the Black Knight may not fight the Knight of the Round Table, nor remove any points.

In order to travel to the centre of the board and fight the Black Baron, a Knight of the Round Table must first land on a castle immediately prior to moving to the centre of the board.

The traps

When a player lands on:

An unoccupied trap, he must miss his next turn.

A trap occupied by another Knight of the Round Table, he must miss his next turn.

A trap occupied by the Black Knight, he automatically loses one point and misses his next turn.

If the Black Knight lands on a trap already occupied by a Knight of the Round Table, he automatically removes one point from that Knight. Experience points can only be removed once from a Knight in this way throughout the duration of that particular stay in that trap.

If a Knight of the Round Table possesses no experience points and the Black Knight lands on a trap occupied by that Knight, then an extra turn must be missed by the Knight of the Round Table.

If a Knight of the Round Table lands on a trap with a throw of six, he must forfeit any further throws, remain in the trap and miss a turn.

A Knight of the Round Table may be sent to the nearest trap and miss a turn if he is attacked by the Black Knight but has no points to lose.

BATTLES WITH THE BLACK KNIGHT

When the Black Knight lands on a square other than a castle or trap, which is already occupied by a Knight of the Round Table, battle immediately begins. If more than one Knight of the Round Table occupies that space, the Black Knight engages both Knights individually in battle.

Similarly, when a Knight of the Round Table lands on a square other than a castle or trap, which is already occupied by the Black Knight, they must immediately start to battle. The battle must be completed before the player makes the dice throw to move the Black Knight.

Battle rules

The Knight of the Round Table rolls one die.

The Black Knight (another player is chosen to represent him for the battle) rolls a second die.

The highest roll wins the battle.

BLACK BARON'S STRENGTH .... POINTS

	Order of play		EXPERIENCE POINTS							
RED KNIGHT	2									
ORANGE KNIGHT	2									
YELLOW KNIGHT	2									
GREEN KNIGHT	2									
BLUE KNIGHT	2									
PURPLE KNIGHT	2									

Fig 29.1

The points which the Knights of the Round Table gain and lose during the game are recorded on an experience card, as shown above.

If identical numbers are rolled, further rolls are made until there is a winner.

Outcome of the battle
If the Black Knight loses, the Knight of the Round Table retains all his current points.

If the Knight of the Round Table loses, the Black Knight removes two points from the Knight.
If the Knight of the Round Table only has one point at the start of the battle, the Black Knight removes that final point and sends the Knight to the nearest trap, where he must miss a turn.

If the Knight of the Round Table has no points at the start of battle, no battle ensues and the Knight is sent to the nearest trap, and must miss a turn.

To prevent battle
A Knight of the Round Table can buy off the Black Knight by automatically letting him remove one point.

BATTLE WITH THE BLACK BARON

Using his own judgement, a player may decide to engage the Black Baron in battle at any time during the game.

To do this, the Knight of the Round Table must first move to the centre of the playing board. This move can only be made on the turn after he has landed on a castle. To reach the centre, the correct number must be rolled on the die. Whilst progressing to the centre, the player still rolls for and moves the Black Knight as before.

Immediately after a Knight of the Round Table enters the centre of the board, battle commences.

Battle system
Another player is nominated to roll the dice for the Black Baron. Each player rolls two dice.

The total score of the Knight of the Round Table's dice roll is added to his experience points.

In the same way, the total score of the Black Baron's dice roll is added to his strength.

The resulting highest total wins that round.

The first player to win three rounds is the victor in this battle.

Outcome of the battle

If the Knight of the Round Table wins the battle, he has saved the land and won the game.

If the Black Baron wins the battle, the challenging Knight can no longer participate in the game, and the land must be saved by one of the other Knights.

Example

Knight (9 points)	Baron (8 points)	
Dice roll 6 + 2 Total 17	5 + 3 Total 16	Knight wins
Dice roll 4 + 3 Total 16	2 + 1 Total 11	Knight wins
Dice roll 4 + 1 Total 14	6 + 5 Total 19	Baron wins
Dice roll 3 + 3 Total 15	4 + 3 Total 15	Draw
Dice roll 6 + 3 Total 18	5 + 2 Total 15	Knight wins

The Knight of the Round Table defeats the Black Baron and wins the game.

CONSTRUCTION

Game board 12mm ($\frac{1}{2}$in) birch plywood 380mm ($14^{15}/_{16}$in) diameter circular board. It is advisable to construct a simple jig to assist with cutting out the game board and marking its various circles. This jig, made from 3mm ($\frac{1}{8}$in) plywood, measures 216mm ($8\frac{1}{2}$in) × 25mm (1in) × 3mm ($\frac{1}{8}$in) – *see* Fig 29.2.

Drill a hole near to one end to act as the centre point of the game board. This hole should be slightly smaller in diameter than a panel pin to enable free, but positive, movement when a pin is tapped through.

O   *Hole for biro*

•   *Hole for pencil*

+   *Point for panel pin*

Holes are drilled at intervals along the length of the jig, to coincide with the required circles on the game board; these holes need to be of different diameters.

The inner two circles and outer two circles on the game board are marked with a biro. It is important when drilling the hole to ensure that the biro nib will only just poke through, thereby producing a good, consistent line; a sloppy fit gives no control. It may be necessary to counterbore the hole with a larger size bit to achieve this.

The outer circumference of the actual game board and the four circles between the inner and outer two circles are marked with a pencil. Again, ensure that the pencil tip fits the hole snugly.

The underside of the jig should be totally smooth, as any rough edges will scratch the game board's surface.

Sand smooth your chosen piece of plywood and pin the marking jig into position. Do not hammer the pin flush, as this makes it difficult to remove. Draw the circles.

Remove the jig and cut out the game board. This can be done with either a motorized fretsaw, treadle fretsaw, bandsaw or jigsaw (beware of the top grain splitting, as this cuts on the upstroke), or a hand-held fretsaw.

If you do not have access to any of these options, the board can be cut out by making a series of

Fig 29.2
Marking jig.

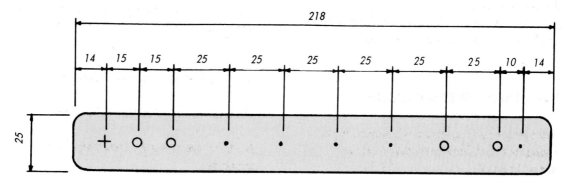

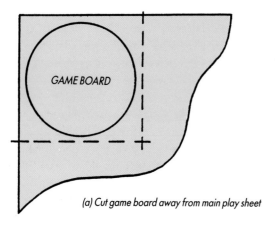

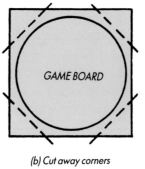

(a) Cut game board away from main play sheet

(b) Cut away corners

(c) Smooth edges for round board

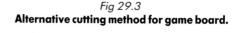

Fig 29.3
Alternative cutting method for game board.

Fig 29.4
Pattern for top half of Black Knight.

straight cuts round the edge with a panel saw; round off the edges with a spokeshave, and finish with a sanding block – *see* Fig 29.3.

The Knights of the Round Table Six 40mm (1⁹⁄₁₆in) clock finials of a suitable hardwood, with their bottom location pegs removed.

The Black Knight 40mm (1⁹⁄₁₆in) clock finial with its top neck and ball plus bottom location peg removed. A chess-style knight is then fretsawed from a similar hardwood, e.g. beech, and attached to the base with glue and a small dowel. Fig 29.4 illustrates the pattern we used. Alternatively, a clock finial, like the other Knights, coloured black, could be used, but this will not look as dramatic!

Dice Two 18mm (³⁄₄in) dice.

MARKING AND FINISHING

With a pencil, lightly mark the straight dividing lines, which are all taken from the centre of the game board. Each line is 10° apart; this can be easily marked using a protractor.

Fill the hole left by the panel pin at the centre of the game board with a suitably coloured filler, and then sand flush.

Using a rule and French curves as necessary, pen over the appropriate lines, as shown in Fig 29.5.

The internal lines of the castles are 5mm (⁷⁄₃₂in) from the outer lines. These can also be marked with a combination of rule and French curves. The three traps are simply marked along the diagonals of the squares.

Remember to erase all pencil lines after the pen marking has been completed.

Mask the areas to be left natural by applying varnish. When this is dry, colour the remaining areas of the game board, including the edge – we used thinned, blue artist's acrylic paint.

The six Knights of the Round Table are stained with various thinned mixes of artist's acrylic paint. The Black Knight is painted with matt black modeller's enamel paint. All the Knights are varnished and green velour is put on to their bases, to protect the surface of the game board during play.

From outer edge inwards:

1st dia.	*380*	*2nd dia.*	*360*
3rd dia.	*310*	*4th dia.*	*260*
5th dia.	*210*	*6th dia.*	*160*
7th dia.	*110*	*8th dia.*	*60*
9th dia.	*30*		

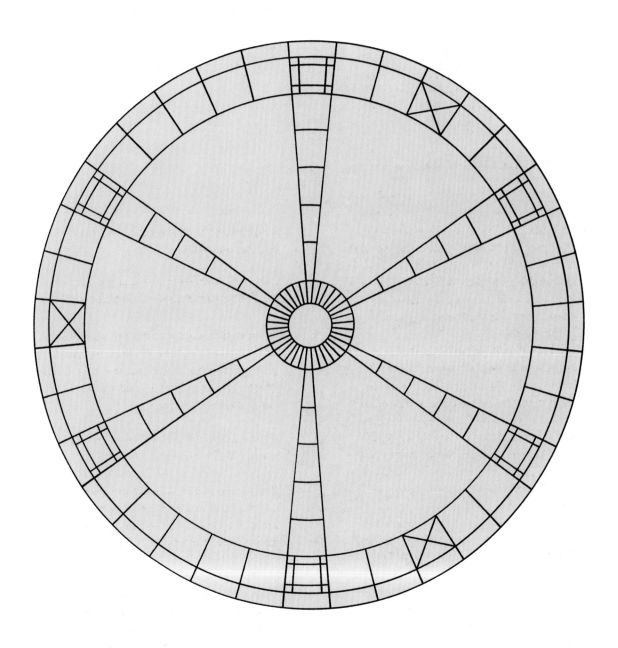

Fig 29.5
Knights of the Round Table game board.

HALMA

INTRODUCTION

Halma was invented in the 1880s and enjoyed great popularity
for a number of years. The name is based on the Greek word
for 'jump'. Although the rules of the game are easy to learn, the
strategy level is high during play; for this reason we have
awarded Halma with a 6 for level of play, but do not be put off
by this, as Halma is great fun to play!

OBJECT OF THE GAME

For each player to move all their pieces across the board from
their starting 'Yard' to the Yard diagonally opposite. The first
player to do so wins the game.

FOR TWO OR FOUR PLAYERS

EQUIPMENT

- Halma game board
- 19 black playing pieces
- 19 natural (white) playing pieces
- 13 red playing pieces
- 13 green playing pieces

PREPARATION

In each corner of the game board is a Yard or Camp, consisting of 19 squares, with a thick green line to mark its perimeter. Inside this Yard is another, smaller Yard of 13 squares: the perimeter of this Yard is marked with a thick red line.

PLAY

Each player may move only one piece per turn. There are two types of move: the 'Step' and the 'Hop'.

The Step is a move of one square in any direction to an adjacent vacant square.

The Hop is a move in which a playing piece may hop (jump) on to a vacant square over another piece which is on an adjacent square, provided that the vacant square is in the same direction. A player may hop over either his own or his opponent's pieces, so it is possible to make many hops in one turn. These hops may be in any direction, provided that each individual hop starts and ends in a straight line.

Two players: one player controls the 19 black playing pieces, the other the 19 natural (white) playing pieces. Each player places his pieces on to the 19 squares contained in their Yard. The Yards must be diagonally opposite each other.

Four players: each player controls 13 playing pieces of the same colour. Each group of 13 playing pieces is placed in one of the four smaller Yards.

Each player should try to tactically manipulate his playing pieces to allow multiple hops; this is called 'creating a ladder'. Of course, the opponent's playing pieces may be used as part of a ladder, and so some highly bizarre zigzagging moves are possible!

When there are four players, play moves in a clockwise direction.

140

CONSTRUCTION

Game board 12mm (½in) birch plywood 340mm (13⅜in) × 340mm (13⅜in).
Edging 21mm (¹³⁄₁₆in) base moulding.
Playing pieces Sixty-four 32mm (1¼in) high hardwood clock finials with their bottom location pegs removed.

MARKING AND FINISHING

After marking, the 256 playing squares are coloured alternate light and dark: on our board, half the squares are left natural and the others are coloured a rich dark brown.

The Yards are marked with green and red lines.

The decorative border is made by being divided into three continuous lines. The middle line is green and 4mm (⁵⁄₃₂in) wide, while the other two are red and 3mm (⅛in) wide.

The edging is left natural.

The game board and edging are varnished.

The playing pieces are stained the following colours:

19 black
19 natural
13 red
13 green

They are then varnished.

Fig 30.1
Halma game board.

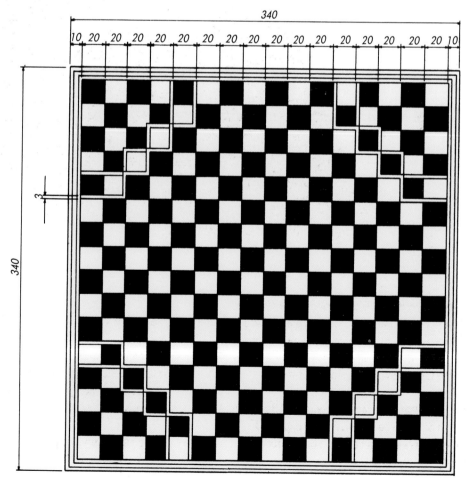

141

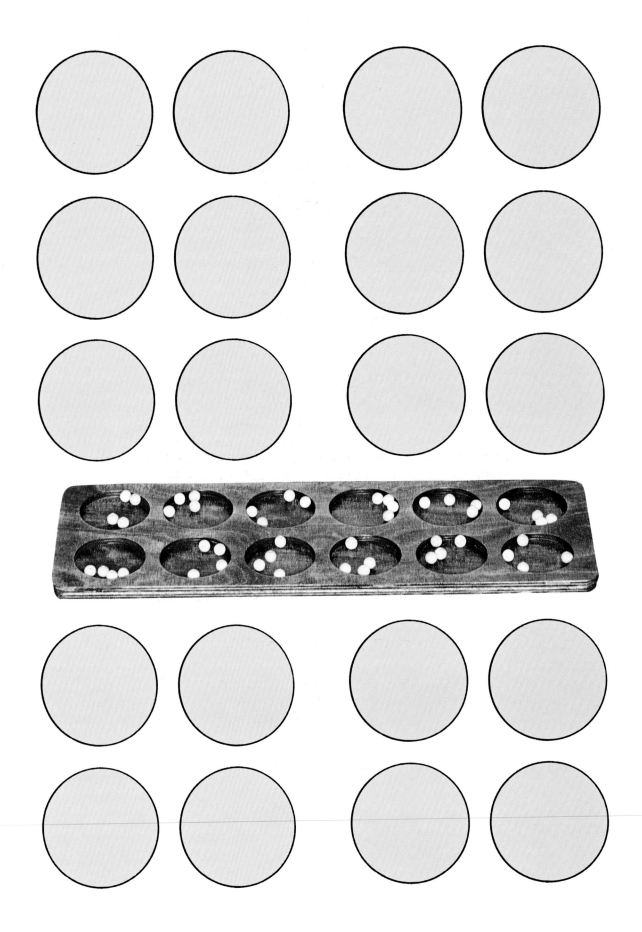

³¹ WARI

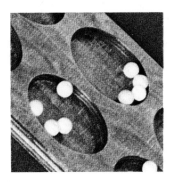

INTRODUCTION

Wari is one of the many games known collectively as Mancala games; these games, which date back thousands of years, probably originated in Africa and Asia, and are still popular in many of the countries in these continents today. The version of Wari shown here is played in Ghana.

Traditionally the game, consisting of two, three, or four rows of cups or hollows, was carved from wood, moulded from clay or simply scooped out of the ground. In all the games the players have to 'sow' counters into these cups or hollows. Pebbles, seeds, shells, and stones were often used for this purpose.

OBJECT OF THE GAME

Each player tries to win as many beads as possible by 'sowing' them around the game board. The player with the most beads at the end of play is the winner.

FOR TWO PLAYERS

EQUIPMENT

- Wari game board
- 48 beads or playing pieces

PREPARATION

Each player owns or controls one row of six pits. Four beads are placed in each of the 12 pits.

PLAY

The first player picks up the beads from any one of the pits in their row and 'sows' them around the game board, one by one, in an anticlockwise direction, starting in the pit immediately adjacent to the one vacated.

Play alternates, with each player in turn emptying one of their pits and sowing its beads.

When the last bead sown in a turn goes into an opponent's pit which, after this sowing, contains either two or three beads, the sowing player wins all the beads in that hole and removes them from the board. If any adjacent pits also contain two or three beads, these are also won and removed from the board.

If a pit contains 12 or more beads, the sowing will complete a full circuit of the board. In this instance, the pit from which the beads are taken is passed over and left empty.

Following a turn which empties a player's row entirely of beads, his opponent must attempt to sow the beads so as to leave at least one bead in that row. If he fails to do so, then he forfeits all his remaining beads. If this is not possible, the game is over.

The game may also end by agreement if a few beads are just being moved around the board, with no player having a chance to win any.

Any beads left in the pits at the end of the game are added to those already won by the player who owns the row in which they are situated.

The player with the greatest number of beads is the winner.

CONSTRUCTION

Game board Two pieces of 6mm ($\frac{1}{4}$in) birch plywood 478mm ($18\frac{13}{16}$in) × 162mm ($6\frac{3}{8}$in).

One piece of plywood has twelve 63mm ($2\frac{1}{2}$in) diameter holes cut into it, forming two even lines of six holes (*see* Fig 31.1). A brace and expansive bit was used to cut the holes. You may find it helpful to drill a tiny pilot hole into the centre of the hole positions before cutting them out: this will help the expansive bit to remain in position while boring.

Hold the plywood firmly in a vice when the holes are being bored. It is advisable to stop boring when you have reached approximately the halfway depth of each hole. Turn the ply around and finish boring from the other side: this will help prevent the surface of the plywood splitting outwards.

When all the holes have been cut, clean them up using a piece of abrasive paper wrapped around a short piece of dowel, 12mm (½in) × 25mm (1in) in diameter.

With both pieces of plywood well sanded, glue them together. When the glue has set, the edges may be cleaned up and the corners rounded if desired.

Beads Forty-eight shop-bought 10mm (⅜in) diameter wooden beads are used. The 6mm (¼in) plywood used to construct the game board enables easy finger access to the beads when 'sown' into the holes. The ease with which the beads can be lifted from the holes should be considered when deciding on the thickness of plywood, and the size of bead, to be used.

MARKING AND FINISHING

No markings are required on the Wari game board, but you may like to add some for decoration.

The game board should be a contrasting colour to the beads used.

The use of a natural wood stain – we used American rosewood – not only highlights the grain pattern of the plywood, but also helps to give the game board a traditional feel. The game board is varnished.

Fig 31.1
Wari game board.

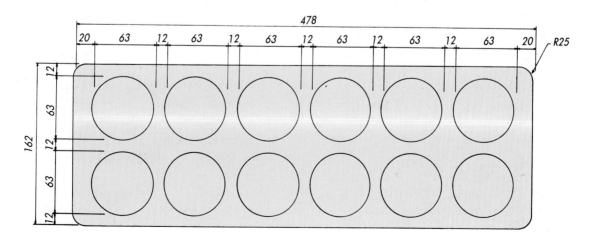

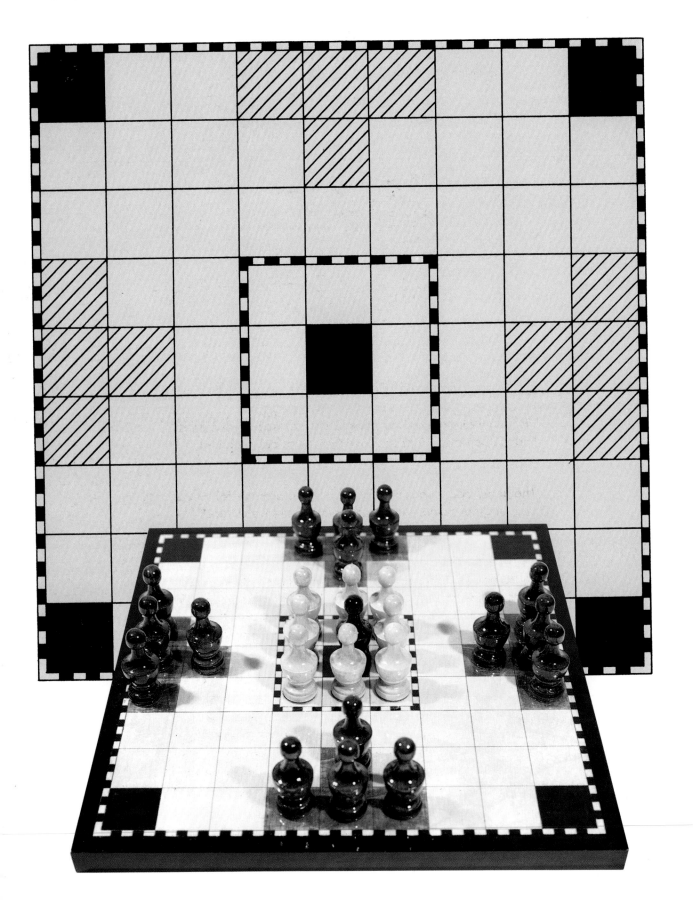

HNEFATAFL

INTRODUCTION

This Scandinavian game dates back to at least AD 400, and documentary evidence shows that it was being played in Britain by AD 925.

The game board shown in Fig 32.1 is a smaller version of the original game, which had a playing area of at least 18 × 18 squares.

As in the games of chess and draughts, tactical play is paramount in playing Hnefatafl, so the design of our game board is drawn from contemporary chess and draught sets. The decorative borders, especially the one that surrounds the centre nine squares, have no bearing on the game and may be omitted if preferred.

OBJECT OF THE GAME

One player controls the King and his eight guards, the other controls the 16 enemy pieces. The King must move, with the protection of his guards, from the centre to one of the corner black squares; his opponent must try to trap the King before he achieves this.

FOR TWO PLAYERS

EQUIPMENT

- Hnefatafl game board
- 25 playing pieces – 1 King (black)
  8 King's guards (natural)
  16 enemy pieces (mahogany)

PREPARATION

The King is placed on the central black square; the King's guards are placed on the eight adjacent squares to the King; the enemy pieces are placed on to the 16 mahogany squares in groups of four.

PLAY

The King's side always moves first, with turns alternating throughout the game.

Each playing piece may move one square at a time in any direction except diagonally. Once play has begun, all playing pieces may move on to any colour square, the only restriction being that the enemy may not 'sit' on any of the corner squares, thus stopping the King from reaching them.

Playing pieces may be captured and removed from the game board by being trapped: a playing piece is trapped when it has an opposing piece on either side of it – again, only in a straight line, and never diagonally.

A playing piece may move to a square between two of its opponent's pieces without being captured, but if one of the opponent's pieces moves away and then back again, the playing piece is considered trapped, and is removed from the game board.

To trap and capture the King, the enemy playing pieces must surround him on all four sides.

If the King reaches a corner square, he wins; if the enemy captures the King before he reaches a corner square, they win.

CONSTRUCTION

Game board 12mm (½in) birch plywood 231mm (9⅛in) × 231mm (9⅛in).
Edging 9mm (⅜in) × 15mm (¹⁹⁄₃₂in) ramin strip.
Playing pieces Twenty-five 32mm (1¼in) high hardwood clock finials with their bottom location pegs removed. Leave these pegs in place until after the playing pieces have been finished — it makes holding them much easier!

MARKING AND FINISHING

The playing area is gridded into 9 × 9 25mm (1in) squares, making the total playing area 225mm (9in) × 225mm (9in).

The decorative border is 3mm (⅛in) wide. To recreate the simple alternating pattern on this border, divide the length of each playing square equally into five.

The 16 enemy squares (the four sets of four squares positioned at the middle of the sides of the board) are stained mahogany, using a wood dye. Before staining, seal the rest of the board with varnish.

Next paint the four corner squares, the central square, and the relevant sections of the decorative borders black.

The edging is also painted black.

The game board and the edging are then varnished.

16 of the playing pieces are stained the same mahogany colour as the enemy squares on the game board. One (the King) is painted black and the others (the guards) are left natural. All the playing pieces are then varnished.

Fig 32.1
Hnefatafl game board.

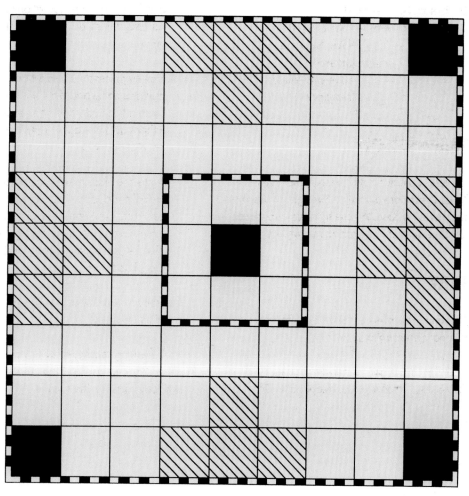

GLOSSARY

CONSTRUCTION, MARKING AND FINISHING TERMS

Butt joint A simple joint where the two items to be joined are placed together, with no interlocking parts, and fixed.

End grain After cutting across the fibres (or grain) of a piece of wood, the new surface exposed is termed the end grain.

French curves Available in various sizes, French curves are flat pieces of transparent plastic with a number of different curved lines and shapes cut into them. Used as an aid to drawing accurate curves.

Gloss finish A highly shiny and reflective finish to paint or varnish.

Jig A device which enables a repetitive operation to be carried out, usually without the need for major adjustment and remeasurement.

Layout The overall placings of the constituent parts that make up the final plan of an item, e.g. game board layout.

Lead screw As in expansive bit. A central, prominent pointed screw that helps guide and pull the bit through the wood accurately.

Marquetry The inlaying of veneers to produce a decorative picture or pattern.

Matt finish A flat non-reflective finish to paint or varnish.

Mitre Where two pieces of wood have been cut at the same angle (usually 45°) and joined.

Moulding In the context of this book, a length of decorative edging usually made up from a series of curves and beads.

Pilot hole A small diameter hole drilled prior to screwing a screw in place or using a large drill bit.

PPI Points per inch: used to indicate the number of tooth points on a saw. The more points per inch, the finer the saw cut.

Satin finish A mid-sheen finish to paint or varnish.

GAME PLAYING TERMS

Banker The person in a game who represents the 'Bank'. In gambling games, the player who pays out or receives the other player's stakes when they win or lose.

Bet A wager or stake.

Counters Similar to gaming chips. Also used as playing pieces.

Defense team The defending team, side or player.

Foul An illegal shot, action, or move.

Gaming chips Handy sized flat discs or rectangles of plastic, card or wood, used as stakes in gambling games.

Innings The period, or periods, of a game where one side or player is batting.

Odds The probability of an occurrence. In gambling games, 'odds' refers to the amount a player may win for his stake. For example, 'evens' means the winning player receives an amount equal to his original stake plus his original stake; 2–1 means the winning player will receive 2 to every 1 unit of his stake plus his original stake. Odds are usually given with a bias in the favour of the Bank (Banker).

Offensive play Attacking play.

Offense team The attacking team or side.

Playing pieces Representative items that are used to record position and movement in a game.

Playing pitch The ground on which a sports game is played.

Pot As in to pot a ball. To pot, or potting a ball, in table games such as snooker, billiards, and pool is where one of the balls has been played into a pocket (a hole at the side of the game table).

Round A round in a game is when all the participating players have each completed one turn.

Stake An amount that has been bet by a player in a gambling game.

METRIC CONVERSION

INCHES TO MILLIMETRES AND CENTIMETRES

MM — millimetres   CM — centimetres

INCHES	MM	CM	INCHES	CM	INCHES	CM
1/8	3	0.3	9	22.9	30	76.2
1/4	6	0.6	10	25.4	31	78.7
3/8	10	1.0	11	27.9	32	81.3
1/2	13	1.3	12	30.5	33	83.8
5/8	16	1.6	13	33.0	34	86.4
3/4	18	1.8	14	35.6	35	88.9
7/8	22	2.2	15	38.1	36	91.4
1	25	2.5	16	40.6	37	94.0
1 1/4	32	3.2	17	43.2	38	96.5
1 1/2	38	3.8	18	45.7	39	99.1
1 3/4	44	4.4	19	48.3	40	101.6
2	51	5.1	20	50.8	41	104.1
2 1/2	64	6.4	21	53.3	42	106.7
3	76	7.6	22	55.9	43	109.2
3 1/2	89	8.9	23	58.4	44	111.8
4	102	10.2	24	61.0	45	114.3
4 1/2	114	11.4	25	63.5	46	116.8
5	127	12.7	26	66.0	47	119.4
6	152	15.2	27	68.6	48	121.9
7	178	17.8	28	71.1	49	124.5
8	203	20.3	29	73.7	50	127.0

ABOUT THE AUTHORS

Jeff Loader's childhood passion for devising, adapting and playing with toys and games has never ceased.

Leaving playing aside for a period, Jeff developed his other interest — woodwork, eventually combining the two by designing and making wooden toys.

In addition to his own workshop, Jeff set up and ran a toy-making department for a children's charity, which donated the toys to children with special needs. Here the challenge of adapting toys to meet the specific needs of the children was combined with teaching woodworking skills and practices to beginners.

At present he is concentrating on designing games and toys for publication as projects. This serves the joint purpose of satisfying his creative instinct and also his desire to share the joy of producing items which will, hopefully, become treasured and much used.

Jennie Loader has a keen interest in many aspects of art and craft, and pursues this interest when time allows. Her working life has always involved children — first as a manager of a charity which specializes in undertaking drama and creative play activities with special needs children, and now as the organiser of a children's out-of-school sports coaching association.

Jeff and Jennie were both born in the West Country and live with their young son, Luke, in Glastonbury, Somerset.